FINANCING INFRASTRUCTURE

Innovations at the Local Level

Prepared by Apogee Research, Inc.

for the

National League of Cities

December 1987

Funding for this project was provided by a grant from E.F. Hutton and Company.

Washington, D.C. 20004
ISBN 0-933729-30-8

Price: $10.00 per copy to NLC members
$15.00 per copy to Non-members

Please add $2.00 for postage and handling.
Special rates available for multiple copies.

CONTENTS

PREFACE

Building, maintaining, and operating basic infrastructure are central and continuing concerns of municipal governments of all sizes in all parts of the nation. As the national association of all of America's cities and towns, the National League of Cities is very pleased to present Financing Infrastructure, a volume whose purpose is to assist municipalities in their efforts to provide and pay for those facilities efficiently and equitably.

This book is one product of NLC's on-going research activities. The idea for Financing Infrastructure developed directly from an earlier study of capital finance decision-making in cities. That report, How The Public Works, was published in 1986 and was researched and written by Dr. Michael A. Pagano of Miami University who held NLC's Lincoln Government Fellowship for 1985-86. Readers of this book may also be interested in more information about the effects of Federal tax policy on local finance. NLC recently published Your City's 1040, an analysis and guidebook for city officials who want to figure out the effects of the 1986 Tax Reform Act on their locality. We will also soon release another study by Dr. Pagano, The Effects of the 1986 Tax Reform Act on City Finances, which reports on a survey of cities regarding their adaptations to TRA in 1987. The important role that providing infrastructure plays in local economic development is one of the major findings of Tools and Targets: The Mechanics of City Economic Development. This is one of two major reports, released in November by NLC, written by Dr. Ann O'M. Bowman of the University of South Carolina who held the Lincoln Government Fellowship for 1986-87.

Financing Infrastructure makes significant contributions to our understanding of the nature and variety of local capital finance. We commend the authors--Dr. Richard R. Mudge and Dr. Susan Jakubiak, President and Senior Economist respectively of Apogee Research, Inc. in Bethesda, Maryland-- for their hard work and their achievement. We join them in acknowledging and thanking the many people who contributed to the success of this project, especially the municipal officials who provided information about the financing techniques described here.

We especially thank E.F. Hutton and Company which provided a grant to the National League of Cities Institute to make this study possible. We greatly appreciate their continuing interest in improvements in municipal financial practice.

Publication of Financing Infrastructure, reflects NLC's commitment to providing research, education, and other assistance to municipal officials who seek to serve better their cities' residents and to improve the art and science of local governance. We are very pleased to offer this book to municipal officials, to state municipal leagues, and to others who also seek these goals.

Alan Beals
Executive Director

William E. Davis, III
Director, Office of Policy
Analysis and Development

AUTHORS' ACKNOWLEDGEMENTS

The authors received help from many individuals. Most obviously, and most importantly, are the many public officials in the cities and communities we used as case studies. Without exception these individuals went out of their way to explain what they had done, to provide us with background documents, and to share their enthusiasm with us. Their names are listed after each case study (along with addresses and phone numbers). We also thank the many other public officials who responded to our requests for information on local infrastructure financing. Space and time limitations meant we could not include every success story in this book.

Special thanks are due to Dr. Michael A. Pagano of Miami University who helped identify possible case studies, provided considerable help in developing the evaluation criteria in Chapter II, and offered valuable comments at all stages of preparing the book. We are grateful for the sound advice and support provided by the staff of the National League of Cities. Dr. William R. Barnes, Director of Research for the National League of Cities, deserves special mention for his role in conceiving of the project as well as for the practical advice and insights in completing the book. Dr. Kenneth I. Rubin and Mr. Russ Brodie, our colleagues at Apogee Research, provided useful comments and practical help in preparing the book. Help in identifying possible case studies was provided by Mr. Douglas Porter of the Urban Land Institute, by Dr. Peggy Cuciti of the University of Colorado, and by Ms. Nancy Minter, Manager of the League's Municipal Reference Service. Ms. Sherry Snyder edited the manuscript. Ms. Pam Callison of the National League of Cities prepared the final manuscript for publication.

Dr. Richard R. Mudge Dr. Susan Jakubiak

EXECUTIVE SUMMARY

Most public works services have traditionally been provided by local governments, most obviously the nation's cities. In recent years, financial responsibility for infrastructure has increasingly become their burden as well. Local governments now provide half of the more than $100 billion spent each year to build, maintain, and operate our systems of public works -- up from 38 percent 20 years ago. The budgetary pressures faced by federal and state governments mean this financial burden will continue for the foreseeable future.

This burden has encouraged cities to find new ways to finance the public works services required by their residents and by local businesses. The results reflect the imagination and hard work of city officials. This book presents some of these new techniques, describes how they work, how they were implemented, and suggests where else they could be applied.

The 24 case studies were selected to illustrate a range of financing techniques well suited to infrastructure expansion and rejuvenation. Examples cover almost every category of public works and a wide range of local conditions, including central cities, suburbs, and low-density areas. The hope is to encourage cities to use their entrepreneurial spirit to adopt and adapt these approaches. To this end, criteria are presented that can help local officials decide which ideas best fit their particular problems.

While many of the techniques described in these case studies are drawn from Sunbelt cities or fast-growing suburbs, their potential is much broader. In fact, they can be adapted to fit most cities and virtually every type of public works. Most importantly, these techniques are generally not restricted by rates of growth or population density. While some -- impact fees and TIF districts for example -- depend on new development, others are suitable even in communities with no growth. Many will work in largely rural areas as well.

The techniques described in these case studies are grouped into four categories:

- **Special Financing Districts**: distinct geographical areas created within a political jurisdiction in order to raise funds from property owners for specific purposes. These include special assessment districts for initial investment as well as maintenance, and tax increment financing (TIF) districts in areas that anticipate significantly higher property values due to development.

- **Exactions**: money, land, or construction services that a developer or property owner provides to a public jurisdiction. Examples include exactions negotiated as part of annexation agreements, ad hoc developer contributions to expedite projects, and systematic impact fees that fund development-based infrastructure expansion.

- **Utilities**: independent public corporations established to finance, construct, operate and maintain public works. This approach parallels that usually used for electric power and water works. What is unusual, however, is its extension to other public works areas such as stormwater systems and local roads.
- **Public-Private Partnerships**: working relationships in which public and private interests share ownership, or certain features of ownership, in public works. Examples range from direct private investment and operation of a public work facility to ideas such as the sale of water and wastewater treatment capacity rights to private firms and individuals.

These approaches generally rely on user-based financing so that burdens can be allocated proportionally among beneficiaries. In effect, users of public works services may be thought of as purchasers of a specific publicly organized service or product.

The ideas presented here can handle needs of all sizes, including projects that measure in the tens of thousands of dollars or hundreds of millions. They can generate one-time payments, or a stream of funds that pays for operating costs or supports a bond issue.

The choice among financing techniques depends in part on the type of infrastructure to be funded and on consideration of the evaluation criteria described in Chapter II. Of course, none of the approaches is without drawbacks. These disadvantages must be balanced against the need for funding and the realization that no funding at all would lead to even greater disadvantages to an area's long-term economic and social health.

Infrastructure is a vital tool of economic growth and public health. The question is not whether infrastructure should be funded but rather how best to do so. The clear message of the 24 case studies is that there are few technical limits on how public works can be financed. Success requires political, managerial, and technical cooperation. By including examples from all types of public works and from widely varying local conditions, this report can serve as a handbook to help city officials increase their list of potential financing tools.

I. INTRODUCTION

In recent decades, a declining portion of the nation's resources has been used for public works. This reflects a more general national trend toward spending on consumption and away from savings and other forms of long-term investment. The resulting decay in the condition and physical capacity of our nation's infrastructure has been traced in many reports.

Few studies, however, have sought to identify what is being done to stave off this decay, where it is being done, and what the implications are for other regions or other levels of government. As is often the case one must look to local governments for the most innovative ideas.

In particular, very few analyses have looked at how various financing techniques have been implemented. The absence of this analysis is a matter of practical concern; how has the **physical** reality of increased demand been translated into the **political** reality of increased or more effective financing? This book addresses these concerns through a sampling of actual cases.

The focus is some 24 case studies of the specific use of innovative financing techniques by local governments. Most of these case studies are of cities; all involve one or another category of public works; and all represent examples that could be used by cities to help finance the construction or operation of local public works. (In fact, the ideas presented here are not limited to cities, but, in most cases, could be used by other local and state governments).

While the case studies selected cover all regions of the country (see map), no attempt has been made to achieve a uniform geographic distribution. Rather, the focus has been on ideas that have yet to achieve widespread use. Thus, there are few examples of impact fees, since this technique has already been discovered by most municipalities.

For a variety of legal, administrative, and political reasons, many of these newer ideas have been concentrated in a few states -- California, Colorado, Florida, and Texas stand out. This does not mean that they are suited only to these states, or even suited only to fast-growing communities. Rather, one of the lessons learned from examining the cases as a whole is that, in some form or another, almost every technique could be applied in almost every type of community in the country. Imagination -- and in some cases, state or local laws -- represents the key barrier.

ISSUE OVERVIEW

With the phase-out of General Revenue Sharing, and the imposition of more stringent restraints on the accessibility of the tax-exempt debt market through tax reform, the federal government is reducing the availability of financial assistance. At the same time, localities in general and municipalities in particular have had to bear an increasing share of the costs of public works facilities without any concomitant financial assistance. The

MAP: LOCATION OF CASE STUDIES

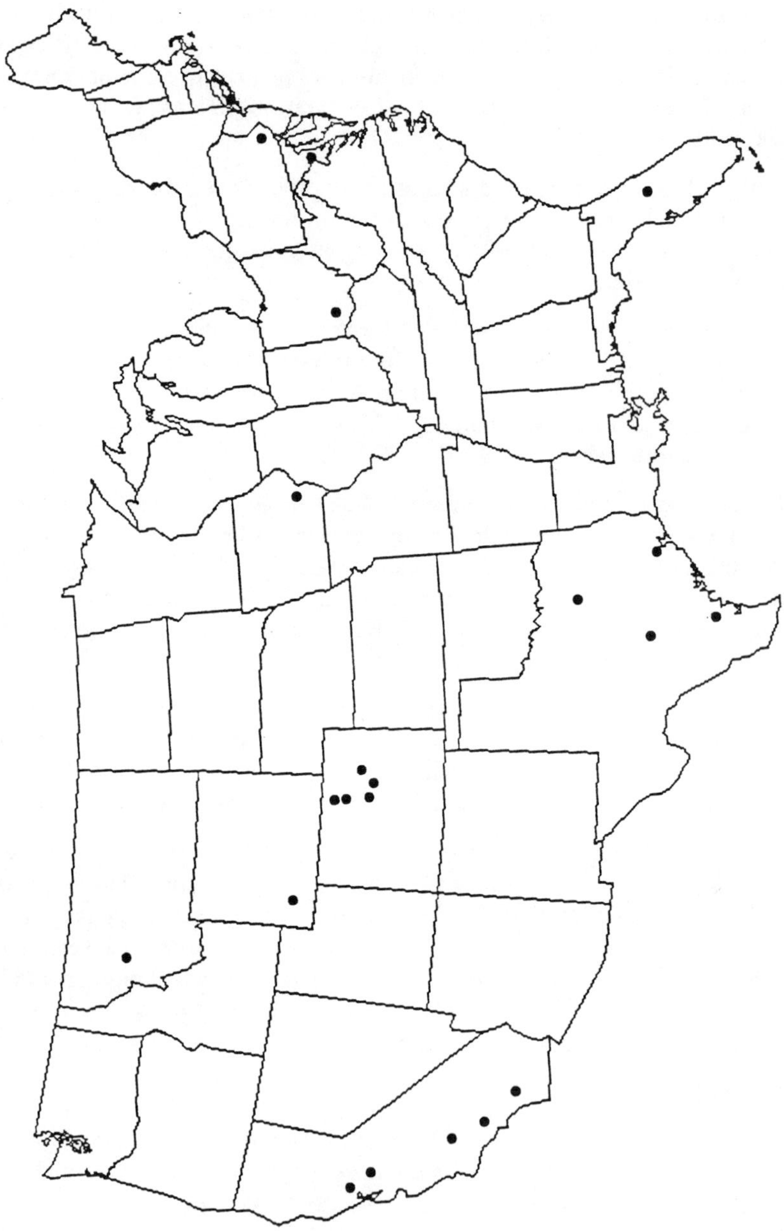

implications have been realized through the development of new financing strategies.

This chapter defines public works infrastructure, discusses investment trends in public works and their impact on the economy, and identifies how the cities' financial role has changed in response. It then concludes with a discussion of the implications of all these factors for local investment policy and a summary of what has been done.

WHAT IS INFRASTRUCTURE AND WHAT DOES IT DO?

Public works projects establish the physical network upon which the country's economy depends -- its infrastructure. This network is not an end in itself. Rather, its importance to the economy and to society as a whole derives from the services it offers: the opportunity to improve productivity or reduce costs. Although most easily thought of in a physical form -- a bridge, a wastewater treatment plant, a subway train -- the real output of infrastructure is service: the movement of people and goods; the provision of adequate clean water. Thus, two measures of the efficacy of the existing system can be contemplated: the investment in physical resources and the services provided by that investment.

For the purposes of definition and assessment of facility condition, the physical traits are considered: what they cost and how they are similar. For the purposes of analysis of the economic benefits of infrastructure, however, the service provided must be considered: how they function to facilitate economic growth.

Definition

Most public works infrastructure projects share several characteristics:

- High investment costs (capital intensive);
- Long economic life and large operations and maintenance costs;
- Potential to dominate local markets; and
- Interaction with other infrastructure projects.

Because of their long time horizon and high construction costs, major infrastructure investments usually involve higher risks than does the more typical industrial investment project. This means that some public-sector involvement is often required. Construction periods are substantially longer than most business investments: three to five years or more is common. As a result, construction costs increase: for example, interest costs capitalized during construction can reach one-third or more of total investment costs.

Most infrastructure projects are part of a larger system -- a national road network, a regional water supply system, etc. The required coordination means that some public involvement is needed even if projects are financed privately. Also, because of the high costs of market entry, many infrastructure projects have near monopoly power in their local market. As a result, economic and safety regulations are often required.

Facilities with these general characteristics -- strong links to economic development, high fixed costs, long economic life, interaction with other parts of a system, and strong traditional public-sector involvement -- may be termed public works infrastructure. This definition usually includes the following "mode:" highways, public transit, water resources, wastewater treatment, water supply, and airports and airways.*

Recent Financial Trends

Total public spending on infrastructure has grown steadily over the past 25 years, increasing fourfold. When measured in constant dollars, spending still increased by more than 60 percent. However, these overall trends mask the ultimate distribution of the implicit increase in the financial burden. In fact, when analyzed by level of government, only one level has borne an increasing burden -- the local level.

Two trends in particular demonstrate the gradual shift in financial responsibility to one dominated by local governments in general, and municipalities in particular. The first trend is simply that of total outlays by level of government (Figure 1). Since 1977, local government outlays have continued to rise, while those of state and federal governments have fallen. The result has been an increasing shift in responsibility away from the state and federal level toward local levels (Figure 2).

As shown in Figure 3, the second trend identifies a broader shift in public works investment, but one that has important ramifications for localities: while funds devoted to capital investment have not kept pace with increases either in economic activity or in population, public spending to maintain and operate the nation's infrastructure has grown in line with the growth of the economy as a whole and has increased almost twice as fast as the growth in population.

The nature and magnitude of investment at all levels of government has shifted dramatically since 1960. Both shifts, however, hold the same implications for local governments, which have had to assume an increasing degree of responsibility for infrastructure investment. Yet, with this responsibility comes the need for a larger revenue base, and, thus, the need for a new technique to generate revenue.

* Except for the lack of strong current public involvement, other areas would fit the infrastructure characteristics set out here. These include communications and railroads. Other observers might include a broader list: government buildings, housing, prisons, hospitals, education, et-

Figure 1. Total Public Works Outlays by Level of Government (Billions of 1984 Dollars)

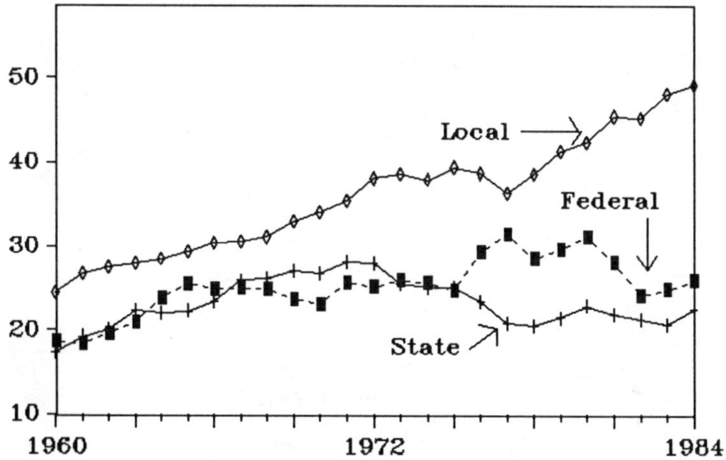

Figure 2. Public Works Outlays by Level of Government – Percent of Total

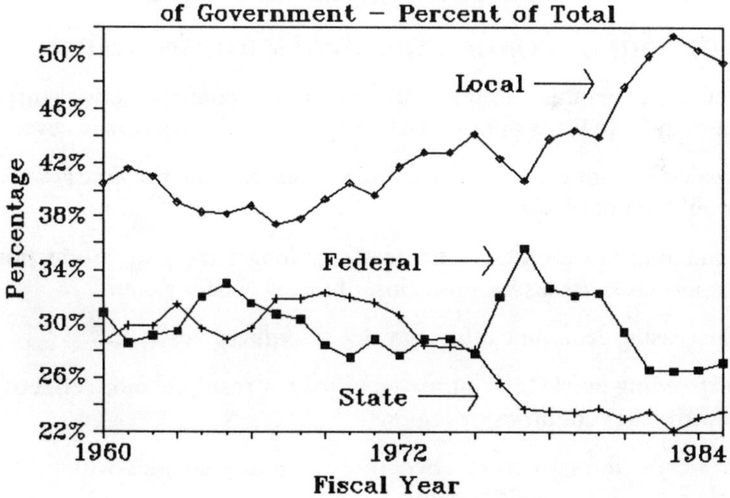

Source: Apogee Research from Bureau of the Census and Budget of the United States Government, various years

Figure 3. Public Spending on Infrastructure

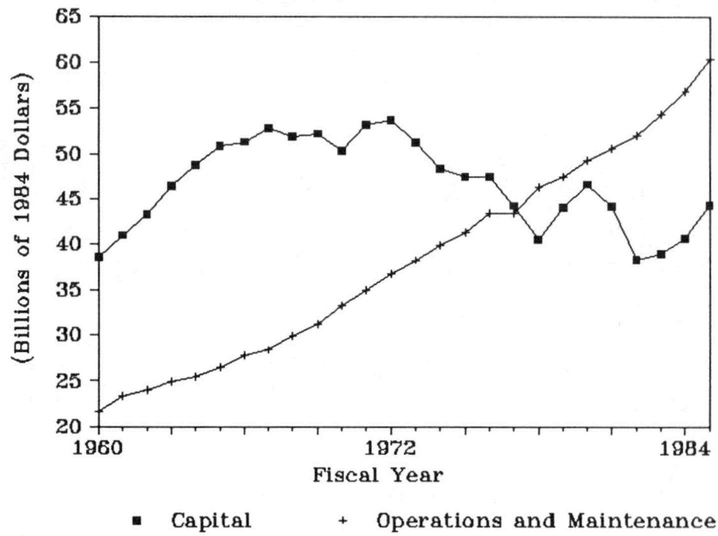

Source: Apogee Reasearch from Bureau of the Census and Budget of the United States Government, various years

ROLE IN FOSTERING ECONOMIC GROWTH AND EMPLOYMENT

Infrastructure generates additional investment or economic activity through a multiplier effect on private firms or other public agencies. This occurs in several ways.

- By making better use of **underutilized resources** that previously were very costly or difficult to obtain;
- By enabling more efficient **trade-offs** among factors of production: reduced transport costs versus location closer to markets, for example;
- By increasing economic efficiency due to **reduced costs**; and
- By **expanding markets** as improved efficiency results in more effective competition with other countries or regions.

In other words, infrastructure encompasses those activities without which there would be only limited economic activity.

Types of Effects on Economic Growth

Users of inadequate facilities bear significant costs. Every time a bridge is closed to traffic or subjected to weight restrictions because of deterioration, users' time and money are lost. In the worst cases, there may also be substantially increased safety risks. Airport delays, mostly occasioned by congestion at large commercial airports, cost the airlines and their passengers more than $3 billion. Similarly, deterioration of pavement on the nation's highways results in substantial increases in vehicle operating costs. For example, operating costs for small automobiles are almost one-third higher on poor roads than on well maintained roads.

Deterioration of existing facilities and insufficient capacity to accommodate future growth will eventually constrain economic development. The nation's transportation network, water supply, and wastewater treatment facilities provide vital services both for industries and individuals; where capacity is inadequate, growth will be stunted. Similarly, a community with badly deteriorated roads, bridges, or other transportation facilities is in a weak position to attract new businesses. Though difficult to quantify, the costs of lost opportunities are no less real.

For example, halting deterioration in the nation's highway network (but not eliminating all deficiencies) would improve economic growth for the economy as a whole, with national income 3.2 percent higher by 1995, employment 2.2 percent higher, and inflation 8 percent lower than if road conditions had continued to deteriorate as in the late 1970s.*

Implications for Local Capital Investment Policy

The existing division of responsibility among local, state, and federal governments derives largely from past history and political forces. Traditionally, local governments (including special districts) have planned, built, and operated most of the nations's public works (exceptions include many highways and most water resource facilities). Significant financial help has been provided by federal and state governments. In recent years, state funds for public works have declined while federal aid has not kept up with growing infrastructure demands. While still playing the dominate operating role for most public works, local governments now must shoulder a larger part of the capital costs for new construction and major rehabilitation of infrastructure.

This book describes some of the responses by local officials and public works managers to these pressures. The case studies presented in Chapters III, IV, V, and VI offer practical demonstrations of what can be accomplished by ingenuity, hard work, and cooperation. Transferring these ideas to other cities requires more than just a good idea. Success requires cooperation among different political forces as well as coordination of a wide range of analytical skills. Chapter II presents a framework for organizing these cases that can help local officials and managers adapt some of these ideas to solve their own local problems.

* Transportation Systems Center, **Highways and the Economy**, prepared for the Federal Highway Administration (November 1983).

II. BACKGROUND ON FINANCING TECHNIQUES

With the financial constraints imposed in recent years by reduced federal grants coupled with taxpayer revolts, local jurisdictions have been forced to generate new ideas to help finance infrastructure. Different approaches have been tried for a variety of public works investments and in a wide range of local environments. Most of these new techniques shift the financial burden away from the taxpaying base at large and toward the individuals and firms who benefit directly from the new or improved infrastructure. That is, most of these approaches rely on user-based financing.

This book identifies financing options and describes their unique characteristics; case studies were selected to show the components of each approach in greater detail. This chapter defines the major types of approaches and notes their most important features, discusses the major public policy issues involved in the selection of financing options, and describes the primary administrative characteristics of each approach. Each of the next four chapters focuses on a particular approach, including several case studies that illustrate how the technique has been applied.

FINANCING APPROACHES

The case studies presented here belong to one of four basic groups:

- **Special Financing Districts** -- distinct geographical areas created within a political jurisdiction in order to raise funds from property owners for stated needs.
- **Exactions** -- money, land, or construction services and materials provided by a developer or property owner to a public jurisdiction.
- **Utilities** -- independent public corporations established to construct, operate, and maintain public works.
- **Public-Private and Equity Arrangements** -- working relationships in which public and private interests share ownership or certain features of ownership in public works.

Special Districts

Special financing districts are areas created to fund specific projects within the district. District projects are financed either through **extra fees** collected in addition to regular jurisdiction-wide property, sales, and income taxes (**special assessment districts**) or through a **diversion** or earmarking of taxes to a project fund (**tax increment financing districts**).

While state and local legal requirements vary, creation of special districts involving extra fees (**special assessment districts**) usually requires some form of prior approval by district property owners -- a simple majority of owners, for example, or agreement by owners who control a majority of the land area, or owners responsible for a majority of the fees assessed. Thus, unless mandated to protect public health or safety, such incremental fees are essentially self-imposed or sanctioned by the landowners themselves.

Characteristically, once such a district is approved by the required proportion of landowners, participation in special assessment district financing is mandatory for all landowners. One exception is Fort Collins, Colorado, where district supporters can only negotiate repayment arrangements with non-supporters, but cannot force their involvement against their will.

Landowners involved in special assessment district financing may be residents desiring infrastructure improvements, developers interested in readying property for major projects, or commercial establishments helping to fund improvements expected to enhance local economic activity. In general, assessments are based on those property attributes that are assumed to be directly proportional to benefits enjoyed by the property owners.

Special assessment districts can be independent of the local government, having nearly complete autonomy to finance, construct, and manage specific projects. Or, they can be dependent extensions of the local government created only to raise revenue for projects administered by the local government.

Tax increment financing (TIF) districts are a unique form of special district in which no additional fees are collected from landowners; funds for defined programs are raised by diverting part of regularly-assessed property taxes to special project accounts. Revenues equal to those collected in the base year (prior to growth and new development) continue to be deposited in the jurisdiction's general fund. Any increment in tax revenues, however, is deposited in a special fund for debt servicing (e.g., on revenue bonds floated) or otherwise reimbursing the local community for growth-promoting investments made.

TIF districts are financial extensions of the government jurisdiction that created them; they are not politically independent. District revenue is dependent upon increases in assessed property values; thus such districts are suitable when significant development or redevelopment is anticipated.

The advantage of special financing districts is the close and clearly visible tie between the infrastructure constructed or maintained and those who pay for it. A particular advantage of special assessment districts is the flexibility allowed. Assessments can be tailored to circumstances; for example, they can be at the same rate for all within the district or can vary if it is felt that benefits vary among participants according to location or other variables. One argument in favor of uniformity is that variations are more likely to lead to disputes.

In districts that base fee assessments on property attributes such as land area or street frontage, the relative burden of each type of property remains unchanged. Assessments based on area of finished buildings or property value, however, shift the relative burden over time from undeveloped property to developed property. This may place an undue strain on those landowners in the forefront of development, particularly if other landowners lag behind more than expected. If such disparities are accompanied by economic recession, some landowners could be forced into bankruptcy if assessment levels are too great. Indeed, an entire special assessment district may be forced to declare bankruptcy, as has happened recently with some districts in Texas (see Chapter III on special financing districts for details).

Disadvantages of special assessment districts include the likelihood of altering the economic decisions that would have occurred without such fees. These market responses to innovative financing are discussed in more detail below. TIF districts are not characterized by this disadvantage since they do not involve additional fees. A disadvantage of all special financing districts is the possible perception that property owners within the district are receiving preferential treatment in the form of new or improved infrastructure. This may be particularly true for TIF districts in which district landowners pay taxes at the same rate as the general population (see comments by officials in Prince George's County Maryland, noted in the applicability section of that case study below).

Exactions

Exactions may be generally defined as money, land, or construction services and materials provided to a public jurisdiction by a developer. A developer may offer exactions voluntarily to expedite project approval or completion. Or, exactions may be an "entry charge" required by local jurisdictions as a prerequisite for building. In this case, charges may be negotiated individually or assessed on a systematic basis according to an established formula legislated by local or state authorities. In the latter case, developers are required to pay impact fees or special taxes to compensate the local community for provision of off-site services and infrastructure in addition to any on-site infrastructure required by local building codes.

Traditional exactions include land dedications for rights of way, parks, and the like, and cash payments in lieu of land. Exactions have been expanded in recent years to include donations of specified facilities, construction of off-site infrastructure such as intersections and roads adjacent to the development, addition of low- or moderate-income housing units to the development project, and impact fees.

Impact fees differ from special assessment district fees in three major ways:

- Revenues from special assessment districts are restricted geographically, while impact fee revenues may be used anywhere in the collecting jurisdiction;
- Impact fees for all new entrants in the jurisdiction are fixed at the same rate, whereas fees in assessment districts may vary within the same district and from district to district within the same jurisdiction; and
- Impact fees are imposed by the local jurisdiction and do not require prior approval by participating landowners.

Specified impact fees often follow a period of negotiated exactions. When exactions are negotiated, individual circumstances can be considered -- the desirability of the project or the developer's ability to pay, for example. However, negotiations take time, outcomes are uncertain, and variations among exactions may create ill will among developers as well as the public. The use of standardized impact fees has the advantage of equality of treatment, but at the expense of flexibility. The move to impact fees usually occurs because the administrative ease and equality of treatment of impact fees is considered more advantageous than the flexibility of negotiated exactions.

In both cases, a successful program of exactions requires strong demand for development in a given area or else a community content to suffer reduced growth to maintain a balance between demand and supply of infrastructure. The advantage of exactions of all kinds is the ability to shift at least part of the burden of development to the new entrants that create the infrastructure bottlenecks.

Utilities

Utilities are a type of independent special assessment district created to oversee all aspects of a particular public works system including financing, construction, and operations and maintenance. They are autonomous public corporations answerable to local governments. Utilities may be distinguished from other independent special assessment districts by their greater duration, geographical breadth, and functional scope.

Utilities are not created for a limited duration such as the infrastructure construction period but are assigned perpetual responsibility to operate and maintain the particular public works facility. In addition, utilities are not established for selective neighborhood components of a public works system; the whole generating and distribution structure is usually included. Finally, utilities handle all decisions concerning financing, personnel, and administration directly; these decisions are not delegated to another governmental department.

Most public works utilities charge one-time connection fees for capital costs plus regular monthly or annual fees for operations and maintenance. Some utilities also assess periodic capital fees along with user fees. The base unit used to calculate each fee depends primarily on the particular public works involved.

Utilities function well in both high- and low-growth areas. Their advantage is in allocating costs on the basis of use of the particular public works system and, because of their autonomy, in insulating their expenditure and long-term planning decisions from the uncertainties of general revenue budget pressures. The ability of utilities to adequately provide for capital needs depends on the fee structure instituted; the impact on development itself depends on market response to fee rates and types.

Public-Private and Equity Arrangements

While most of the financial techniques discussed in this book involve public-private cooperation, some rely on direct participation by one sector (public or private) in a venture controlled by the other sector. In these cases, funds or services are contributed in exchange for enjoyment of certain rights or future income.

Private participation in public works can be active or passive. Active participation includes direct private investment and administration of a basically public responsibility such as the Babylon, New York, solid waste processing plant in which a private firm contributed part of the initial capital and administers the leased facility under the city's overview.

There are several types of passive private participation in public works. In the first, private developers or new entrants contribute funds in exchange for contractually defined rights to use the public works being constructed. The advantages of these arrangements, such as sale of sewer and water access rights, is the contribution to capital by those needing the incremental capacity and a corresponding shift in burden away from users already in the system. As with many other financial instruments, disadvantages include the possibility of altering development decisions.

In the second type of passive private participation, investors "own" a specific public works facility through their purchase of certificates of participation or equipment trust certificates -- financial instruments backed by physical assets. The infrastructure itself is held by a trustee as collateral, and the user makes lease payments which, in turn, are used to pay debt service.

Unlike general obligation bonds, certificates do not require voter approval. Thus, local jurisdictions can save time, money, and avoid possible voter rejection. This is particularly important when required funding is small compared to the costs of voter approval. Moreover, some authorities (for example, some transit districts) cannot issue bonds but can issue certificates backed by equipment.

Certificates can be issued only to finance physical capital that is suitable as collateral and only in jurisdictions in which local authorities are allowed to negotiate long-term leases. Therefore this approach is not universally applicable. Like other bonds, it is a means to bridge the gap between immediate need and future revenues; it is not a resource-generating approach. Thus, repayment methods must be evaluated at the same time as the use of certificates is considered.

Public equity or equity-like involvement in private undertakings is less common. Characteristically, a public political unit (municipality, for example) is assigned a portion of the gross or net revenues from a private venture as payment for government property sold or public services rendered to the venture. Government thus becomes a partner in the private profit-making project in return for its aid in establishing the project.

One disadvantage of this approach is uncertainty concerning a revenue stream that cannot be controlled or altered by the local jurisdiction. The advantage to the public at large is in being relieved of some portion of the cost of infrastructure provided to economically viable private ventures. The private venture gains because repayment to the public depends on future profitability.

Summary

The dividing lines between these four financing categories are not hard and fast, and one category often shades into another. Indeed, components of each approach are found in other approaches, and some instruments could be redefined and placed in another category. For example, fees paid by members of special assessment districts are a form of exaction, and utilities can be seen as a more narrowly defined type of independent special assessment district.

Although some instruments are used more in some situations than others, most are generally applicable and can be modified to suit individual circumstances. The search for the perfect financing approach will be in vain. Rather, there is a list of options, each with some unique characteristics, not all of them suitable in the same form for all situations.

Conceptually, financing options can be presented in a matrix with instruments listed down one side and columns for each factor that might influence the choice of instruments. In the following discussion, the factors relevant to the choice of financing instruments are segregated into two areas: public policy considerations and administrative characteristics.

PUBLIC POLICY CONSIDERATIONS

When analyzing the various tools available for private-public partnership in financing infrastructure, public officials must keep in mind the public policy implications associated with innovative financing in general and each instrument in particular. Two considerations are primary:

- **Fairness or equity** -- equality in treatment of different groups of landowners and/or residents, including: equity between new entrants and established landowners/residents or between residents in special financing districts and all others (called inter-group equity); equity within a given group such as new entrants (intra-group equity); and equity between current participants and future generations (intergenerational equity).

- **Market sensitivity or elasticity** -- sensitivity of development decisions to fund-raising approaches introduced to finance public works, primarily a developer's alteration in plans in response to additional charges levied for development in a particular area and for development of a particular type.

Fairness

Established residents often state that "growth should pay its own way." In other words, it is not fair to tax the current population to provide infrastructure necessary for new entrants. Rather, those who benefit from this new public capital should bear the added financial burden. Approaches perceived as fair are most likely to be feasible politically and to survive legal challenges.

Equity or fairness is an elusive goal. Most controversy focuses on "inter-group" equity and "intra-group" equity, which are forms of horizontal equity or equity between participants at a single point in time. A third concept is intergenerational equity or fairness over time between residents and entrants active now and future generations of residents or developers not yet involved.

Inter-group equity concerns the degree of fairness achieved between established residents and new entrants or between landowners in special financing districts and those outside. A key factor in inter-group equity is whether or not the benefits of the new development to established residents will themselves outweigh the associated infrastructure costs they might be asked to finance. Some argue that the net benefit is negative, that the incremental costs are greater than the benefits enjoyed, and therefore some degree of financial support is required from new entrants and developers. An answer to this question depends on a careful identification and evaluation of the costs and benefits. This process, in turn, is vital to the choice of financing approach and the levels at which fees are set.

Intra-group equity concerns the degree of fairness among different developers or new entrants themselves. The form of private-public financing can directly affect equity among new entrants. Perceptions of unfairness can increase public resistance to innovative financing and/or influence the forms of financing selected by public officials. Individually negotiated agreements in particular can create problems unless variations can be rationalized by differences in infrastructure costs or local benefits provided rather than by differences in bargaining strength.

For example, before many jurisdictions in Florida enacted across-the-board impact fees based on number of units built, only the larger developers were assessed fees to help underwrite supporting infrastructure since it was felt that smaller developments could be absorbed without expanded capacity. But this policy created problems, in part because the cumulative impact of the small developers was certainly not inconsequential yet they made no financial contribution comparable to those made by large developers.

Intergenerational equity. Although the current generation of users may have caused a shortfall in infrastructure capacity, it is not clear that they should be held responsible for the full costs of expansion since future generations of users will also benefit from these investments. Thus, the selection of financing instruments and the proportion of investment costs recouped from the current generation are affected by considerations of intergenerational equity.

Equity or fairness does not necessarily mean equal burden per unit or per acre; equity in general requires that each infrastructure user pay either in proportion to the impact resulting from his demand or, alternately, in proportion to the benefits received. Equity, therefore, is open to interpretation. Table 1 summarizes some of the objective characteristics of each financing instrument relevant to considerations of equity.

Just as each kind of development creates different impacts, some private-public financing tools are considered more equitable than others. However, there is more than one definition of equity, and some instruments satisfy one definition but not another. For example, **special assessment districts** involve a close geographical association

Table 1 - Public Policy Considerations: Factors Relating To Equity

	Equity Among New Entrants		Equity Between New Entrants and Established Residents	
Financial Approach	Within Special District	Within Full Jurisdiction	Within Special District	Within Full Jurisdiction
SPECIAL DISTRICTS				
Assessment District	YES	NO	YES	NO
TIF District	YES	YES	YES	YES
EXACTIONS				
Negotiated	NO	NO	NO	NO
Impact Fees	YES	YES	NO	NO
UTILITIES				
Capital Fees				
One-Time	YES	*	NO	*
Recurring	YES	*	YES	*
User Fees	YES	Probably	YES	Probably
EQUITY ARRANGEMENTS				
Private Equity				
Active Involvement	N.A.	N.A.	N.A.	N.A.
Passive Involvement				
Certificates of Particicipation	**	**	**	
Access Rights	YES	*	NO	NO
Public Equity				
Profit Sharing	NO	NO	NO	NO

* Depends on the number of operating areas - one large area with uniform charges or several smaller areas with individual facilities and finances.

** Depends on how funds are collected to pay debt service.

between fees paid and infrastructure financed, thus providing an equitable allocation of burden within a specifically defined area.

On the other hand, **impact fees** are imposed at the same rate for all developers in the jurisdiction regardless of location or cost of infrastructure immediately adjacent to each development. **TIF districts** ensure equality of assessment for both established residents and new entrants. Nonetheless, this approach may be considered inequitable by those who feel that new entrants should pay for at least a portion of the incremental infrastructure needed with fees as well as regular property taxes.

Utility user fees are considered fair because they are based on actual consumption and because the same rate is charged to both established residents and new entrants in the same utility service area and, usually, throughout the whole utility system. Utility capital fees can be set at the same rate for all new entrants or at different rates for each service area within the utility. In this regard, they are similar to general impact fees and special assessment district fees, respectively, and have the same characteristics of intra-group equity.

In contrast, **negotiated exactions** focus on maximizing private contributions to public works, with little attention paid to fairness. Similarly, negotiated profit-sharing arrangements are not necessarily equal for all participants. Certificates of participation may or may not satisfy fairness conditions, depending on how debt service funds are raised.

When designing private-public financing of infrastructure, public officials first must define equity as they perceive it. Second, they must decide whether equity is a primary consideration and, if not, what other considerations take precedence. That is to say, they must determine to what degree they are willing to trade off equity in order to achieve other goals.

Fairness is not likely to be the sole criterion in selecting among financial options. For example, public officials must consider the economic and financial impact on the community at large of each new development and its importance to the community. This, in turn, requires officials to evaluate the impact of the approaches chosen on development itself.

Market Sensitivity

Public finance always takes into consideration the effect of innovative approaches on potential new entrants: how are economic decisions likely to change in response to the amounts developers are required to pay? Of the financing instruments considered here, only tax increment financing is likely to be neutral with respect to developer response. All other options place some additional financial burden on new entrants -- fees, special assessments, purchase of access rights, or utility capital fees.

Unless developers are insensitive to the type and level of financing approach, public officials must balance the goal of increased private contributions to infrastructure financing with the need to attract new growth and development. There are three areas in which the level and type of innovative financing may affect the response of new entrants, thus having an impact on local community environment as well as its financial situation.

- **Market entry**. If the additional burden imposed by innovative financing is considered too great, developers may choose to relocate to another jurisdiction with lower "entry" fees. The decision to continue development or abandon the project altogether is a function of **demand elasticity**; the decision to remain in a given community or move the project to another community depends on **elasticity of location** or the strength of commitment or preference the developer has for a given locale.

- **Project size and mix of uses**. Even if project location is unaffected, fee structure and level may influence the final outcome. For example, payments based on acreage may encourage developers to increase land use density thus minimizing fees per unit. They may also redesign a development to favor commercial space over residential. The degree of developer sensitivity determines the influence that infrastructure financing policies will have in shaping the projects themselves.

- **Land and development prices**. Rather than reduce profits, developers will naturally try to reduce the burden of infrastructure cost-sharing, either by passing the costs **forward** to final customers (home buyers, commercial renters, etc.) or **backward** to landowners from whom they buy property for the project. The ability to pass infrastructure costs forward depends on the strength of demand for the final product (residential housing, commercial space, etc.). If demand is strong and fairly insensitive (inelastic) to price increases, the incremental costs can be passed forward to final users without much effect on demand. The ability to pass costs backward by paying less for land depends on the elasticity of land supply -- how much land is available at various prices. If landowners are anxious to sell or land is readily available in suitable blocks, then it will be easier for developers to pass infrastructure investment costs backward and force land prices down.

Local officials must balance their need to pay for incremental infrastructure with the effects such exactions may have on the nature, volume, and prices of development itself. But they must do this without precise knowledge of the elasticities involved.

The characteristics of various financing approaches as they relate to elasticity or market response are shown in Table 2. Both the instruments chosen and the base-unit selected to assess fees may influence development size and characteristics. Since any addition to regularly assessed taxes can turn away new development, only TIF districts are unlikely to affect entry decisions. Once a developer has decided to accept additional "entry" costs, innovative financing approaches will probably not affect development size unless there is a threshold below which developments are not assessed.

Innovative financing, however, can affect development **design**. Although ad valorem fees are unlikely to influence design, fees based on physical attributes of the project may

Table 2 - Public Policy Considerations: Factors Relating to Elasticity

Financial Approach	Basic Unit for for Fee Assessment	Entrant Response May Be Influenced with Respect to:		
		Entry into Area	Development Size	Development Type
SPECIAL DISTRICTS				
Assessment District	Land area	YES	NO	YES
	Number and type of building units	YES	NO	Possibly
	Street frontage	YES	NO	YES
	Assessed value	YES	NO	NO
TIF District	Assessed value	YES	NO	NO
EXACTIONS				
Negotiated Exactions	N.A.	YES	YES	YES
Impact Fees	Land area	YES	*	YES
	Building units	YES	*	Possibly
	Street frontage	YES	*	YES
	Assessed value	YES	NO	NO
UTILITIES				
Capital Fees				
One-Time Charges	Anticipated consumption or building units	YES	NO	NO
Recurring Charges	Consumption	Maybe	NO	NO
User Fees	Consumption	Maybe	NO	NO
EQUITY ARRANGEMENTS				
Private Equity				
Active Investment	YES			
Passive Investment				
Certificates of Participation	**	**	**	**
Access Rights	Anticipated consumption	YES	NO	NO
Public Equity				
Profit Sharing	Actual income	YES	NO	NO

* Only if there is a distinction in fees between large and small projects.
* * Depends on how funds are collected to pay debt service.

do so. For example, distinctions in assessment among developments of different types (commercial, industrial, residential) may affect the final project mix.

Furthermore, development **density** may be altered in response to additional fees levied for infrastructure. All development entails basic costs that depend on the land area involved but not on the number of units built -- the fixed costs of land acquisition and preparation, for example. Any increase in the number of units or square feet built on a given land area spreads these fixed costs over a greater volume and thus reduces the average cost per finished unit. Any fee based on land area or lot frontage is an added incentive to increase density to spread these additional costs. Even fees assessed per unit or per square foot of finished space can influence density if there is strong pressure to maintain a given average cost per unit. Increased per-unit costs due to fees can be mitigated by increasing the number of units or square feet built per acre, thus spreading fixed costs over a greater number of units.

The effects of innovative financing on developer decisions (entry, development type and design) depend not only on the instrument selected but also on the base-unit chosen for assessment, the differentiation in treatment by development type (commercial, residential, industrial), local zoning constraints, and market conditions. Figure 4 presents a simplified example of the dilemma faced by public officials.

In this situation, Developer A is willing to pay a high fee per acre ("$oe") to underwrite infrastructure costs associated with this development; Developer B is willing to pay less per acre, perhaps because the development is of lower density or land was purchased more recently and at higher cost; and Developer C has the lowest limit ("$ob"). (Quantities are represented by line segments described by their endpoint. Thus, "$oe" is read graphically as the distance between the origin, point o, and point o, and point e on the dollar axis of the graph).

If this hypothetical jurisdiction established an across-the-board impact fee of "$oc" per acre, Developers A and B would continue with their project plans, but Developer C would cancel his plans in this community. At a fee level of "$oe," only Developer A would continue with his plans; and at any fee level above "$oe," none of these developers would be interested in pursuing projects in this community. On the other hand, at a fee level of "$ob," all three developers would proceed with their plans and "ov" acres would be developed. At any lower fee level, the local jurisdiction would lose funds it could have obtained without any change in development acreage.

Clearly, in this hypothetical example, public officials could have charged higher fees than "$ob" to Developers A and B.

But if all developers are charged the same fees, the city is forced to choose between higher fees with less development and lower fees with more development. Moreover, they must make this choice without precise information on developer preferences or tolerance for additional fees. They may overestimate developer willingness to pay such fees and thus aim too high with a fee that drives away desired development. Conversely, they may underestimate developer willingness to pay such fees and set fees so low that

Elasticity: Effect of Price on Development

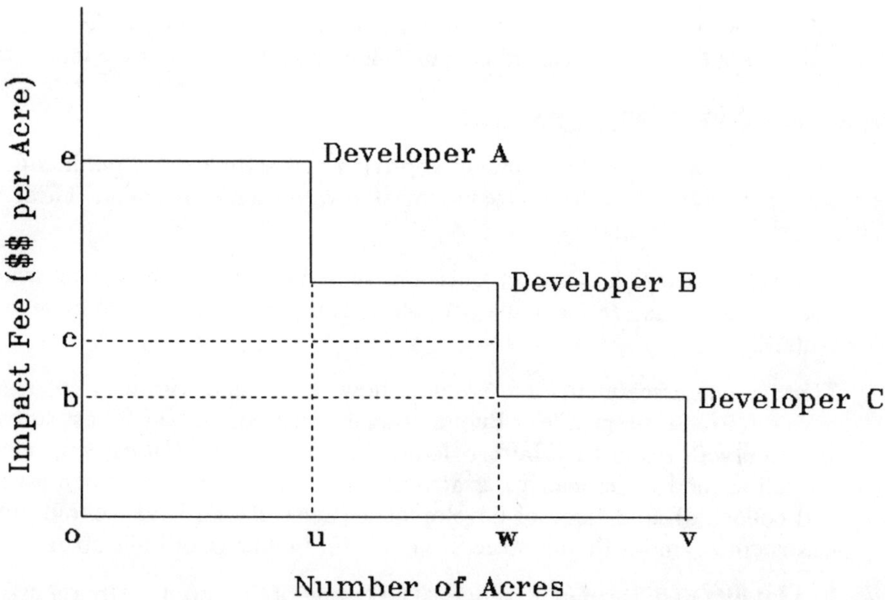

Figure 4

response is beyond expectations and development is excessive in the context of an overall plan.

There is another choice that allows greater control: different exactions negotiated with each developer. A wily public board with some feeling for the elasticities involved could exact the limit from each of the three developers, thus maximizing support for infrastructure without jeopardizing development plans. In economic jargon, this would be called skimming the "developer surplus" for each project.

On the other hand, this aggressive policy would clearly erode conventional forms of equity. Thus, attempts to minimize the impact on decision-making and maximize private payments clearly conflict with the goal of achieving fairness among developers. Again, there is no single right answer; public officials must weigh these factors in their choice of financing mechanisms and the levels at which fees are set.

Considerations of market sensitivity are relevant to all financing policies discussed in this book except tax increment financing in which no additional fees are introduced.

ADMINISTRATIVE CONSIDERATIONS

In selecting the appropriate financing approach and setting rates, public officials must consider the administrative factors associated with each instrument. Three subjects are particularly relevant:

- **Cost Basis:** Before fees are set, decisions should be made on how to allocate infrastructure costs. In particular, should fees be based on average or marginal costs?
- **Timing:** The assessments and revenue flows associated with each instrument have different time profiles. Public officials must decide which best suit their situation with respect to: infrastructure expenditures (initial capital, ongoing operations and maintenance), exactions (one-time or ongoing, when assessed and collected), and stage of development (undeveloped land without any infrastructure, land with infrastructure ready for buildings, or built-up area).
- **Bondability and Form of Revenue:** The timing of the revenue stream may not match the timing of expenditures required for a particular infrastructure investment. Bonds are one way to translate future revenues into funds today.

Economic Basis for Calculating Costs: Average Versus Marginal

Some infrastructure costs are so closely tied to a particular development that it is easy to calculate the project's fair share--for example, the costs of tying in to the main water distribution system or building a connecting road. And, on-site costs are clearly the burden of the particular development. In many cases, however, a project's fair share of off-site infrastructure is less easily specified, particularly when there is no easy way to tailor the capacity exactly to the immediate demand created.

As an established community reaches the capacity of its infrastructure, the addition of one small development project will force the system beyond its physical capacity, requiring an expansion of off-site facilities. In most cases, such expansion cannot be made in small increments but requires a basic minimum level of investment -- a whole new wastewater treatment plant or an extra highway lane. Public officials may choose however to sacrifice some economies of scale and expand capacity in smaller units, as Houston does with area-based treatment plants, but investments are nonetheless lumpy.

The question then arises as to how new entrants are to be assessed their fair share of the costs of such expansion. Should new development pay the full cost of expansion, that is, the full **marginal cost**? Or should each user of the system -- old and new -- pay an equal portion of the costs of expansion, thus assessing new entrants only their proportion of the **average cost** of the whole system? If marginal cost pricing is used, should new development pay for the whole "lump" of investment, or only the share that is required now?

This situation can be shown graphically (Figure 5). Assume a community in which highways currently have peak-hour capacity of "om" vehicles per hour. A new suburban development will require highways with a total capacity "op" vehicles per hour. The efficient provision of this capacity requires more highway capacity than needed by the new development alone -- expanding a two-lane arterial to a four-lane arterial, for example -- thus creating surplus capacity of "ps" vehicles per hour available for future use. The current (two-lane) highway system costs "$oa," but the expansion in highway capacity (four lanes) to "os" will cost "$ac," bringing total cost to "$oc." How should this incremental cost be allocated?

Under **average cost** pricing, all users would pay "$oc" divided by "op" ("$oc/op") apiece per unit of capacity. On the basis of **marginal cost** pricing, new entrants who cause the crisis in capacity would shoulder the burden of "$ac." They might be asked to pay a maximum of "$ac/mp" per unit apiece, thus bearing the full cost including that of the excess capacity ("ps" vehicles per hour). More probably, they would be assessed an **"average" marginal** cost of "$ac/ms" per unit, thus paying for their share of the incremental capacity ("$ab"); new (future) users would be charged for the balance ("$bc") as they arrived on the scene.

Of course, as in the example on developer fees, introduction of fees can have a feedback effect on the number of infrastructure users that actually materialize. For example, if the fees are set at the average marginal cost of "$ac/ms" per unit and charged to the developer who occasions the traffic bottleneck, the developer may reduce the size of the development or alter its configuration so that less than an "mp" increase in traffic is anticipated. In light of lower anticipated traffic, fee revenues of less than "ab" would be collected and a greater proportion of road costs would remain unreimbursed.

In order to take advantage of economies of scale in construction while charging developers only the "average" marginal cost, some jurisdictions (Fort Collins, Colorado, for example) encourage oversizing. The cost to construct public works beyond a

Average Versus Marginal Costs
For New Suburban Development

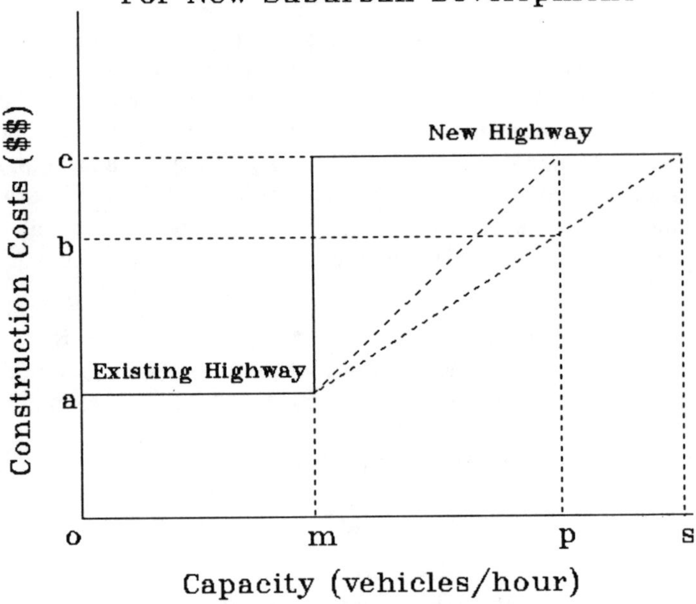

Figure 5

developer's immediate needs is subsequently reimbursed either by the local jurisdiction or by future developers who later enter the area.

Timing

Time affects the choice of financing approach in several ways:

- Time frame for **infrastructure support**: initial capital or the long-term costs of operations and maintenance as well;
- **Maturity and direction of development itself:** raw land or partially or fully developed property, and changes expected in the future time period;
- Time frame of **developer assessments and payments:** whether assessments and payments are one-time or over time; and
- Time frame of **revenue received** by the local jurisdiction including its regularity and predictability.

Table 3 summarizes the characteristics of each approach as they relate to these time-related factors.

Infrastructure support. There are two components of public works financing: initial capital and ongoing operations. Over the short term, raising capital for construction is the prime concern. Most private-public financing arrangements focus on this need, ignoring the annual funds needed for maintenance, though many financing approaches are equally suitable for funding operations and maintenance.

Assessment districts provide a good example. In most cases, they have been used to finance initial capital costs only. But, in Missoula, Montana, and Denver, Colorado, they fund ongoing maintenance as well. Sale of sewer access rights, such as in Escondido, California, is normally used to raise initial capital investment funds. However, if access prices were set high enough, the surplus over initial capital needs could be set aside in a trust to underwrite ongoing maintenance costs.

Maturity and direction of development. The level of expenditure and, to some extent, the type of infrastructure required depend on the maturity of development and on the expected time frame of development. Infrastructure needs are greatest when property is being developed for the first time, and the surrounding infrastructure is relatively undeveloped. Some financing arrangements may be more applicable at different levels of maturity than others. For example, the sale of access rights and the imposition of exactions are more appropriate when property is first developed.

Moreover, some financing instruments are more suitable when high growth rates are anticipated; others are suitable even when no growth is expected. For example, TIF districts can be used only when property values are expected to increase substantially whether in undeveloped areas or developed areas being revitalized. On the other hand, special assessment districts and utilities can be established in non-growth as well as high-growth jurisdictions and at any development maturity level.

Table 3 - Administrative Considerations: Factors Relating to Time

Financial Approach	Infrastructure Support Direction	Development level and Profile	Factors Affecting New Entrant: Predictability	Factors Affecting New Entrant: Assessment	Factors Affecting New Entrant: Payment	Jurisdiction Revenue
SPECIAL DISTRICTS						
Assessment District	Initial capital	ALL	Known recurring	One-time or recurring	One-time installment or recurring	Related to expenditure; irregular
	O&M	ALL	Known with periodic chng.	Regular recurring	Regular recurring	Regular
TIF District	Initial capital	New, growing	Known	Regular recurring	Regular recurring	Expect steady growth
EXACTIONS						
Negotiated Exactions	Initial capital	New, growing	Uncertain	Usually one time	Negotiated	Irregular
	O&M	New, growing	Uncertain	Usually one time	Negotiated	Irregular
Impact Fees	Initial capital	New, growing	Known	One-time	One-time	Irregular
UTILITIES						
	Initial capital	ALL	Known	One-time and/ or recurring	One-time and/ or recurring	Irregular
	O&M	ALL	Known with periodic chng.	Regular recurring	Regular recurring	Fairly regular
EQUITY ARRANGEMENTS						
Private						
Active	Initial capital	N.A.	Negotiated	Negotiated	One-time or recurring	Depends upon
	O&M	N.A.	Negotiated	Negotiated	Negotiated	Arrangement
Passive						
Certificates of Participation	Initial capital	ALL	*	*	*	One-time bond receipts
Access Rights	Initial capital O&M	New, growing	Known **	One-time **	One-time **	Irregular (Regular)
Public						
Profit Sharing	Anything profit	N.A.	Negotiated	Negotiated	Recurring	Depends upon profit

* Depends on source of funds for debt service.

** Operations and maintenance needs can be accomodated with spin-off from trust established with surplus proceeds from one-time payments for access rights.

Developer assessment and payment. There are three dimensions to this issue: the predictability of the assessment or time lapse between development planning and assessment, the time frame of the assessment itself, and the time frame for payment by the developer.

The predictability of assessment depends on the instrument used to finance infrastructure. In a negotiated arrangement, each agreement is unique and no developer can predict with certainty in advance. On the other hand, fees that are applied universally throughout a jurisdiction, such as impact fees or the purchase of utility access rights, are known in advance of project planning.

Many financing arrangements involve a single **one-time assessment**. For example, a special district established to underwrite the cost of a specified road improvement typically makes a one-time assessment in which the total cost is divided among landowners based on acreage or frontage. Similarly, most impact fees are assessed at a single point in time for each development. On the other hand, utility districts may levy annual assessments on each district landowner. A combination is found in Fort Collins, Colorado, which levies one-time fees for new entrants plus ongoing assessments for infrastructure maintenance.

The choice of one-time or ongoing assessment usually depends on whether or not the focus is on initial capital only. However, at least two financing structures -- TIF or tax increment financing districts, and the Texas RUD or road utility districts -- are associated with periodic assessments based on property values to fund initial capital costs only. In these cases, bonding provides the bridge between the time frame for expenditure and for assessment and collection.

The **payment period** may match that of assessment or may be stretched out in time: it clearly can never be less than the assessment time frame. Thus, one-time assessments can be collected all at once, as is generally the case with impact fees. Alternatively, one-time assessments may be paid in installments; landowners in Pleasanton, California, can choose to pay their full assessment in a single lump sum or make payments over the life of the bonds issued (20-25 years) including interest pegged to bond rates. Ongoing assessments may be paid as they are set or in installments--for example, quarterly payment of annual property taxes in TIF or RUD districts.

Revenue received. The time frame over which local jurisdictions receive revenues helps determine how funds are used. Revenue received with some regularity and certainty offers the greatest flexibility. For example, predictable annual payments can be used to back bond issues, thus permitting a larger up-front investment. Alternatively, such payments can offer assured support for maintenance and operations as with the transportation utility in Fort Collins, Colorado. One-time payments, such as most exactions, reduce long-term uncertainty, but they also limit flexibility.

Bondability and Form of Revenue

Financing instruments can be selected so that timing of revenue matches timing of expenditures, or local jurisdictions can also choose to issue bonds to bridge the gap between the revenue and expenditure streams. Thus the ability to use anticipated receipts as security for revenue bonds is an important consideration.

Construction of major infrastructure projects requires a large initial investment that is often not available from public or private sources in time for construction. Bonds provide the means to transform future revenues into funding needed now. Traditionally, only recurring revenues for example, property tax revenues, user fees, and other revenues based on regularly collected taxes or fees have been pledged as security for debt service on bonds issued to fund infrastructure. One-time charges such as impact fees generally have not been considered a predictable and steady enough income source to support bonds. Nonetheless, Orlando, Florida, has used impact fees coupled with debt service insurance to back bonds.

Special assessment districts created to fund construction of major infrastructure traditionally have levied a single lump sum assessment against each property in the district. However, Texas road districts levy annual special taxes; and other districts, such as Pleasanton, California, allow landowners to pay assessments in multi-year installments. In both situations, the expected revenue streams can be used as security for bonds that provide capital funding for the projects. Table 4 describes the bondability of various financing approaches. In most cases, revenues can be used as bond security.

In all the cases included in this book in which bonds were issued to fund infrastructure, income to bondholders was granted tax-exempt status. Under the 1986 Tax Reform Act, eligibility for tax exemption was tightened and greater restrictions placed on the proportion of bond revenues used to underwrite private investment projects. Thus, for example, it is no longer possible to loan the receipts from tax-exempt industrial development bonds to private developers for construction of shopping centers, office buildings, and the like. The Tax Reform Act does not preclude the use of innovative financing approaches described in this book. The Tax Reform Act did, however, create a new regulatory environment. Cities contemplating use of any of these techniques should carefully assess the implications that the Tax Reform Act might have in their particular situation.

In choosing among financial approaches, public officials also need to take into account the form of fee payment -- cash versus land or services. In some cases, it may be administratively preferable for developers to contribute land or construction directly. Further, it may be possible for private firms to provide the public works facility for less than if done through a public contract.

Under negotiated agreements, both for exactions and for equity participation, contributions may be made in cash or may take the form of land for rights of way, parks, school sites, or construction of additional facilities. Special district assessments could be offset by contributions of land or construction services if preferred by the local authorities. Even impact fees, conventionally paid in cash, could be paid in kind. The construction services provided by developers under Houston's Water and Sewer Trust Funds system are contributions in kind by the early developers who are then reimbursed in part from cash (impact fee) contributions made by later developers.

Table 4 - Administrative Considerations: Financial Factors

Financial Approach	Payment Forms		Bondability
	Traditional	Possible	
SPECIAL DISTRICT			
Assessment District	Cash	Cash, in-kind	YES
TIF District	Cash	Cash, in-kind	YES
EXACTIONS			
Negotiated Exactions	Cash, land, construction	Cash, in-kind	NO
Impact Fees	Cash	Cash, in-kind	With insurance
UTILITIES			
Capital Fees	Cash	Cash, in-kind	YES
User Fees	Cash	Cash	YES
EQUITY ARRANGEMENTS			
Private			
Active	Cash, land, construction	Cash, in-kind	NO
Passive			
Certificates of Participation	Cash	Cash	YES
Access Rights	Cash	Cash, in-kind	YES
Public			
Profit Sharing	Cash	Cash	NO

In cases where contributions in kind are substituted for cash payments, the local jurisdiction calculates its cost to provide the services or construction. The contributing developer then receives a credit toward the impact fee or other assessment equal to the calculated cost, regardless of what it actually cost the developer. In all cases, such services must meet relevant state and local standards and criteria to receive credit. The advantage to the local jurisdiction is in bureaucratic effort saved and, perhaps, in earlier completion. The advantage to the developer is in earlier completion and, perhaps, in lower final cost if the developer can provide the services cheaper than the local authorities.

The balance of this book presents case studies that illustrate the use of the financing approaches described above. As emphasized above, no single approach is right for all circumstances. Further, no single approach is clearly better than all others even in particular circumstances. The choice of instrument or instruments depends on both local conditions and local preference. Moreover, instruments can be used in combination which, though probably involving more administrative effort, may be more effective in achieving financial targets and policy goals. Variations on these financing ideas are still being developed. The possibilities are limited largely by the imagination of local officials.

III. SPECIAL FINANCING DISTRICTS

Special financing districts are distinct geographical areas created to raise funds from property owners for stated needs. They may be wholly contained within a local governmental jurisdiction or they may cross jurisdictional lines (for example, Denton County, Texas, Road Utility District). Two basic types of financing districts are delineated, depending on the existence or absence of special fees: special assessment districts and tax increment financing (TIF) districts.

Special assessment districts are defined areas within which extra fees or taxes are collected in addition to the jurisdiction-wide property, sales, and income taxes. This normal increment is most often self-imposed or, at least, sanctioned by the landowners themselves to fund improvements for which public funding is unavailable within the desired time period. That is to say, in cases not involving public health or safety, creation of a district requires prior approval by property owners. The level of approval depends on the laws of the area -- perhaps only a simple majority of the property owners, but sometimes more complex formulas such as approval by owners representing a majority of land area involved or a majority of revenues to be assessed.

In most cases, participation in special assessment district financing is mandatory for all landowners once the district is approved by the required proportion of landowners. A notable exception is Fort Collins, Colorado, where district supporters can only negotiate repayment arrangements with non-supporters but cannot force their involvement against their will.

These landowners may be residents desiring infrastructure improvements, such as in most of the Missoula, Montana special districts; developers interested in readying property for major projects, such as in the Texas road districts and the several special districts in Pleasanton, California; or commercial establishments helping to fund improvements expected to enhance local economic activity, such as in Denver, Colorado and Evanston, Wyoming. Assessments may be limited as in the Missoula districts that maintain street lighting or quite substantial as in the Pleasanton districts that finance new roads and freeway interchanges.

Assessment districts can be independent of the local government, having nearly complete autonomy to finance, construct, and manage specific projects: the Texas road districts, for example. Or, special districts can be dependent extensions of the local government created only to raise revenue for projects administered by the local government.

Special district assessments are based on attributes of the properties that are assumed to be directly proportional to benefits enjoyed by the property owners. However, the basis and level of assessments may vary among special districts even within the same municipality, depending on the needs of each district created and the wishes of participating landowners. Improvements can be funded by ad valorem charges or fees based on such physical characteristics of the properties as acreage, front footage, and use. In

Denver, benefits were assumed to be related not only to the size of the property but also to proximity to the improvement (a transit mall) and thus zones of benefit were defined within the special district with different assessment rates for each zone.

The advantage in using special assessment districts is that the infrastructure investments are funded by those who benefit from them. The disadvantage is possible distortion of market response, particularly in districts involving developers, depending on the form and level of assessments (see the discussion in Chapter II on market sensitivity).

Tax increment financing (TIF) districts are not always grouped in special financing districts but they can be considered as a subcategory since they, like special assessment districts, are created specifically for funding. A TIF district is a specially delineated district within which revenues are raised through ad valorem taxes or property taxes, for example, to fund particular public works.

However, in a TIF district, there are no special fees assessed in addition to regularly imposed taxes. Landowners pay no more in property taxes than they would have paid without creation of the TIF district; rates are the same as for all property owners in the jurisdiction. TIF revenues are from a **diversion** of that portion of property tax revenue attributable to growth. Revenues equal to those collected in the base year (prior to growth and new development) are deposited in the jurisdiction's general fund. The increment over base is diverted to a special fund used to reimburse investors for growth-promoting investments made (i.e., pay interest and capital on bonds issued or repay loans from governmental funds). Since TIF districts do not entail additional taxes, there is no distortion of economic decisions. However, there may be problems of perceived equity as noted in the applicability section of the Prince George's County, Maryland, case study presented below.

In most special financing districts, landowner payments are stretched over time and used for debt servicing of revenue bonds which provide the original investment capital. Financial risk, then, is a function of landowner ability to maintain regular payments. This risk is greatest when repayment is dependent upon economic development to generate the economic base for debt servicing. It is a risk in all special assessment districts where landowners may default on payment of assessments set at high levels in expectations of development; it is a risk even in TIF districts where landowners are not likely to default on taxes due but, because of lower assessed valuation, taxes due will be less than originally anticipated, thus not covering debt service owed by the bond-issuing jurisdiction.

A case in point is the Northwest Harris County Municipal Utility District No. 19 outside Houston, which suspended interest payments due April 1, 1987, on $2.6 million in unrated tax-exempt bonds sold in 1982. The general oil-based economic slump in the Houston area in which this municipal utility district (MUD) is located has prompted the Texas Senate to establish a committee to study the situation of this utility and to determine whether other MUDs are also at risk of default.

PREVIEW OF CASES

The ten case studies included in this section describe districts with varying characteristics to show the range of features possible in special financing districts. Pleasanton, California, has made extensive use of special assessment districts to fund highway access for raw or relatively undeveloped land being readied for industrial and commercial use; assessments are based on land area and are substantial; the amount of land involved is a significant portion of the city's area.

Infrastructure to support future development is also the rationale of special districts in Texas and Davenport, Iowa. Texas' special road districts differ from the other special assessment districts described in this section in two respects: first, they are independent of local governments for the duration of the road building projects and, second, special incremental assessments are based on property values rather than acreage or some other non-varying physical attribute of property. The Davenport, Iowa, special district was also created to fund road building and also uses ad valorem funding but, in this case, the district relies on tax increment financing rather than fees added onto regular ad valorem taxes. Moreover, like most special districts, it is not an independent entity. Prince George's County, Maryland, was among the first jurisdictions to create TIF districts; ten were established before taxing restrictions were lifted and the county moved away from special district financing. It is included as a case study because of its longer history of use.

The Pleasanton, Texas, and Davenport districts are composed of undeveloped land being prepared for development. Special districts, however, can be used for projects in already developed areas. In Missoula, Montana, assessment districts range from neighborhood districts that underwrite limited projects such as streetlights and maintenance to a recent district to underwrite a significant sewer system connector in which tap fees will be used to repay initial capital outlays. The Missoula districts are unique because they include many small-scale projects in established neighborhoods as well as one significant development-oriented larger-scale project, thus demonstrating the versatility of this financing tool even within the same jurisdiction and legislative structure.

Special improvement districts in Fort Collins, Colorado, have many of the same characteristics found in other special assessment districts with one very significant exception: in voluntary special improvement districts, participation is optional and no landowner can be forced to pay assessments voted by the majority even if he will benefit from the proposed investments.

Downtown revitalization was the focus of special districts in Evanston, Wyoming; Denver, Colorado; and Orlando, Florida. In these cases, as in most of the Missoula districts, special districts were created in already developed areas but, in these cases, the downtown nonresidential areas were selected. Evanston is of particular interest since it is a small city; Denver is unique because benefit zones with varying assessments were differentiated. In both of these cities, special districts required payment of fees in addition to regular jurisdiction-wide taxes; these fees were related to property area. Although the ultimate objectives were similar, Orlando's infrastructure for urban commercial redevelopment was funded with a TIF district requiring no increase in fees collected from developers.

The project to build a half-beltway around Denver, Colorado, involves a unique combination of elements found only individually in other special assessment districts. An independent public-private authority was established to oversee construction, financing, and operation of the limited access highway. Although user-tolls are expected to be the primary source of revenue in the long run, the authority also anticipates revenues from special taxes collected from commercial enterprises and developers in the specially defined highway corridor--in essence, a special district that is not coterminous with any other political subdivision. The special assessments may include employee head taxes, sales taxes, impact fees, and additional property taxes.

PLEASANTON, CALIFORNIA SPECIAL ASSESSMENT DISTRICTS

SUMMARY

The City of Pleasanton, California, has made extensive use of special assessment improvement districts to finance bond issues for infrastructure improvements. Pleasanton is a small but rapidly growing community within commuting distance of both San Francisco and Oakland. The city has decided to exploit its favorable location and its proximity to several major highways through development of the area north of the established city. Between 1982 and March 1987, approximately $145 million had been raised for infrastructure (mostly roads) investment in the north Pleasanton area through several individual issues of tax-exempt serial bonds backed by special district assessments.

BACKGROUND

Pleasanton is a residential, commercial, and research center with some manufacturing located approximately 40 miles east of San Francisco; it covers about 14 square miles of land area. Population virtually doubled between 1970 and 1980 and increased another 30 percent by 1986 to more than 45,000. Because of its proximity to San Francisco and Oakland and its easy access to several major highways, Pleasanton expects to experience continued growth in the future.

The area north of the established city is contiguous to several major freeways; although this area includes some buildings, most of the land is not improved and has been targeted for extensive commercial, office, and retail development in the next several years. Currently, there are several business parks and commercial centers in various stages of development. The largest of these is Hacienda Business Park, a mixed-use park of 695 net acres being developed in two phases over 20 years. The area also includes three smaller industrial parks and the 1.2 million square feet Stoneridge Regional Shopping Center mall.

The capital required to develop the nearly 1,000 acres in the north Pleasanton area is large relative to the current population and would constitute a heavy burden if levied directly on its citizens. Moreover, in addition to state-wide restrictions on property tax revenues (Proposition 13), the established population felt that these costs should be borne by those directly benefitting from the improvements, that is, developers and current property owners. In response, the city created special assessment districts to support the bond issues that financed the infrastructure improvements.

PROGRAM CHARACTERISTICS

Special improvement or special assessment districts are based on the principle that the owners of properties that benefit from infrastructure investments ought to be held responsible for funding those improvements. In California, special assessment districts can be created in one of two ways. First, landowners representing 60 percent of the acreage within the proposed district petition the local city council to form a special assessment district. The council holds hearings and may accept or reject the petition. If approved, all landowners within the district become liable for the assessments. Second, the city council may simply declare a special assessment district, and the district will become reality unless landowners representing more than 50 percent of the acreage in the proposed district object.

California law requires only that each parcel of land within an assessment district be assessed for its share of improvement costs in proportion to estimated benefits to be received. No set formula is provided, however, and the benefit formula is devised by the local assessment engineer, subject to approval by the local legislative body, usually its city council.

In Pleasanton, assessments have been in proportion to acreage. Where it is felt that benefits per acre vary within the district, distinctions can be made. In one instance, for example, it was felt that benefits per acre varied systematically according to proximity to road improvements. To accommodate these differences, the city defined separate zones of benefit within the overall district and assessments per acre varied from zone to zone. In some cases, individual exceptions were negotiated with specific landholders, effectively creating mini-assessment districts within a larger district or zone of benefit.

After definition and creation of a special assessment district, the full costs of all improvements, including engineering fees, interest costs, and allocations to the bond reserve fund, are estimated. The bond reserve fund covers possible delinquency in payment of individual assessments. These reserves have ranged from 3 to 10 percent of bond proceeds. The amount assessed against each property constitutes a lien against the property equal to that property's proportional share of expected cost of the improvements.

Property owners have a limited time period in which to choose whether to pay the assessment in a lump sum at the outset of development or in installments. Most property owners in Pleasanton have chosen to pay in annual installments. Infrastructure investment costs are paid for with funds from any prepaid assessments plus the proceeds of a tax-exempt serial bond issue, secured by the unpaid special district assessments plus interest.

The local jurisdiction acts only as a conduit for repayment of bond principal and interest. That is, the annual assessment paid by each property owner exactly equals his share of the bond issue burden. This burden includes annual interest and redemption of bonds falling due each year. Thus, the annual assessment per acre may vary slightly from year to year, depending on the redemption schedule established when the bonds were issued. The interest charged on unpaid assessments equals the interest paid to bondholders.

At any time prior to the final payment, property owners may choose to prepay the balance of their assessment. However, they must pay the full amount that would have been collected during the remaining years (that is, assessments plus interest). The city then decides which bonds to call early with the proceeds of the prepayment. The property owner will then be refunded whatever interest savings remain after the chosen bonds have been called. To date, the prepayment option has not been exercised.

The assessment per acre has varied from bond issue to bond issue. In a district created in 1985, three zones of benefit were defined according to the value of improvements in each zone and the proximity of each parcel to the improved facilities. Assessments against the 62 acres in Zone 1 were approximately $13,700 per acre (net of interest). Assessments for the 275 acres in Zone 3 averaged $25,238 per acre, but some properties were assessed as high as $50,000 per acre. The total outstanding against any one parcel depends on how many times that parcel has been included in special assessment districts and the value of the improvements planned each time--thus the total can be substantial. Some properties included in several previously created districts as well as the new district planned for 1987 will be responsible for up to $200,000 per acre in past and current assessments.

EXPERIENCE

Since 1982, a number of individual districts of varying size have been created in north Pleasanton. Some have been defined as individual business parks; one was delineated as all the areas outside the formal business parks; one consolidated previously defined smaller districts into a larger all-inclusive North Pleasanton Improvement District; and a new 1987 district will include off-site freeway interchanges outside the business parks. Pleasanton estimates that as of March, 1987, it had raised approximately $145 million for improvements in the north Pleasanton area using individual special assessment districts to support bond issues. (Pleasanton had created special assessment districts in other areas in the late 1960s; the revenues involved in each of these were a fraction of those involved in the north Pleasanton area.) This total is net of refinancing used to consolidate and refloat previous smaller issues. Moreover, the city has already cleared the way to raise another $64.7 million in the same manner in the next three years to pay for improved freeway interchanges necessary to fully develop the area.

APPLICABILITY

Special assessment districts have been created in other parts of the country. Individual features vary according to local preference and local and state laws. Most have been created to fund major infrastructure investments as in Pleasanton; others were designed to upgrade or maintain existing infrastructure (see, for example, the case study on Missoula, Montana, presented below). However, all operate through special assessments levied against the property owners who will directly benefit from such improvements. Pleasanton's example stands out among the case studies presented here because of the magnitude of the investments undertaken and the resulting assessments accepted by the landowners involved. Although local laws may constrain the use of special assessment districts in some forms, the greatest restrictions are probably those imposed by landowners unwilling to tax themselves for infrastructure.

Assessments usually vary in proportion to acreage or some other physical yardstick used as a surrogate for proportional benefits. Although neither California law in general nor Proposition 13 in particular precludes the use of ad valorem special assessments -- assessments in proportion to property value rather than acreage or street frontage -- most jurisdictions such as Pleasanton appear to have avoided using ad valorem assessments because they appear to be too closely identified with property taxes. Notable exceptions to this are the several road districts in Texas, described next.

The risk in special assessment districts for development infrastructure, particularly in ones assuming substantial financial burdens like Pleasanton, is that development will not proceed as quickly or be as lucrative as anticipated when the financial burdens were assumed. In extreme cases, if development falls far short of that originally anticipated, and particularly if this is concurrent with economic recession, individual landowners may go bankrupt thus resulting in liens against delinquent properties and/or greater financial burdens placed on the bond-issuing local jurisdiction. The risks associated with special financing districts are discussed in greater detail above in the introduction to this chapter.

REFERENCE

James R. Walker
City Manager
City of Pleasanton
200 Old Bernal Avenue
P.O. Box 520
Pleasanton, California 94566-0802
Phone (415) 847-8008

TEXAS
SPECIAL ROAD DISTRICTS

SUMMARY

Texas law allows the formation of special districts to finance infrastructure investments supported with ad valorem taxes. These are assessed in addition to regular property taxes, and usually support bonded debt service. They are unusual because of their link to property value. There are two main types: road utility districts (RUDs) are formed by the state to support bonds for road improvements; county road districts (CRDs) are formed by a county commissioners' court for the same purpose. The Denton County RUD, the first RUD formed in the state, provides arterial and main feeder routes, an interchange, and storm drainage facilities in a district slated for future development within the City of Lewisville, Texas. Northwest Travis County Road District No. 2 and Southwest Williamson County Road District No. 1 were CRDs created to finance local road construction and improvements in the Austin area.

GENERAL PROGRAM CHARACTERISTICS

There are two types of road districts in Texas: road utility districts and county road districts. Although both are formed to finance road construction and improvements, they differ in formation process and administrative structure. Once completed, infrastructure projects funded through both types of road district are conveyed to the state or the appropriate local jurisdiction. Thus, the government receives new road facilities without paying any of the construction or land acquisition costs; its only obligation is maintenance.

Road utility districts (RUDs) are created by the State Highway and Public Transportation Commission in response to a petition from 100 percent of the landowners in the proposed district. This petition must be accompanied by a letter from the local governing body approving the road project proposed for the jurisdiction and by preliminary financial and engineering plans. The commission holds hearings prior to its decision.

Once created, RUDs are administered by a board of governors composed of district landowners. The initial board is appointed by the state from a list submitted by district developers. As terms expire, subsequent governors are elected by the landowners. Before RUD bonds are issued, they must be approved by the district's registered voters (not simply the landowners). As special district taxes can only be assessed to support debt service on bonds for road construction and improvements, no additional taxes can be levied if bond financing is rejected.

In 1984, the Texas County Road and Bridge Act was amended to expand the power of county commissioners' courts to establish road districts. Although private developers may informally lobby for creation of a particular county road district (CRD), no formal petition is required; technically, CRDs are created by county commissioners' courts on their own initiative.

Moreover, creation of CRDs does not require approval by either registered voters or landowners in a local referendum. However, once a CRD is created, 50 registered voters or a majority of voters (whichever is less) may petition the county to hold an election to determine whether or not bonds will be authorized. In such an election, two-thirds of the CRD's registered voters (not landowners) must approve the bonds. Like RUDs, CRDs can only assess special taxes to support debt service on district bonds; thus no incremental taxes can be levied if bond financing is voted down. In contrast to RUDs which are administered by a separate board, CRDs are administered by the same court of commissioners that established them.

Road districts are political subdivisions of the State of Texas with the power to issue debt to fund road projects and to levy ad valorem taxes to repay that debt. (Legislation passed recently has expanded the basis for fee assessment; CRDs and RUDs are now allowed to assess fees based on factors other than assessed property value.) The Texas constitution, however, limits the total bonded debt responsibility of any given road district to 25 percent of the net taxable assessed valuation of the real property of that district. This limit does not include debt issued by other political subdivisions such as school districts and local municipalities to which the road district properties may also belong.

Bonds issued by road districts are obligations only of the specific districts and not the local municipalities, counties, or the State of Texas. Direct annual ad valorem taxes collected specifically for debt service are the only revenue pledged for repayment. There is no limit on rate or amount of taxes levied and, within each district, tax rates vary according to the assessed value of the properties within that district and the level of debt service. Although the absolute dollar amount of debt service in any district may be fairly constant from year to year, the tax rate necessary to generate sufficient revenue to cover that obligation will vary as assessed valuation varies with economic conditions and development within each district.

BACKGROUND

Denton County Road Utility District

Lewisville, incorporated in 1925, is 30 miles northeast of Fort Worth and 20 miles northwest of Dallas. It is conveniently located on Interstate Highway 35-E only 8 miles north of the Dallas-Fort Worth International Airport. Proximity to these two cities and the airport has provided Lewisville with stable, sustained growth, expanding from a 1970 population of 9,264 to more than 36,000 in 1986. By 1990, population is projected to reach 46,300. Texas Instruments employs 3,300 in Lewisville in engineering, research, and development, as well as production of electronic components.

The strong prospects for continued economic expansion and development of undeveloped property in the Lewisville area created a need for infrastructure improvements to support this growth.

Northwest Travis County and Southwest Williamson County Road Districts

Both the Northwest Travis County and Southwest Williamson County Road Districts are part of the greater Austin area. Situated in central Texas, Austin is 80 miles northeast of San Antonio. It is the Travis County seat and the state capital, as well as a regional education and government center. The April 1986 city population was estimated as 476,000 -- an increase of 33 percent in just five years. It is projected that the population of the Austin SMSA (which includes Travis, Hayes, and Williamson Counties) will reach 818,000 by 1990. Of the approximately 359,000 total jobs in 1985 in the Austin SMSA, 91,000 were in various levels of government; 80,000 each in trade and services; and slightly over 42,000 in manufacturing.

Both districts lie along U.S. Highway 183, which the state highway department has designated for upgrading to freeway status. In anticipation of growth along this corridor, the Northwest Travis and Southwest Williamson CRDs were created to finance construction of roads auxiliary to the newly designated freeway and, in some cases, certain portions of the freeway itself.

Recently, the Austin area has experienced economic setbacks as a result of the decline in the petroleum industry and a recession in the high-tech industry, coupled with a cutback in state government spending. In spite of these setbacks, landholders in the two county road districts are sufficiently optimistic about development in their area to undertake the financial responsibilities associated with issuing bonded debt. There are two major property owners in the Travis CRD, holding approximately 38 acres usable for commercial development. Under existing zoning, 2.2 million square feet of building space could be constructed. To date, 43 percent of the total development capacity has been proposed for medical, health care, and athletic facilities scheduled for completion in 1989.

Property owners in the Williamson County District also anticipate development. The district currently is devoted to low-density uses, primarily agriculture and ranching, with some low-density commercial establishments and a single-family residential area. The 25 homeowners in the residential area recently sold their property to a developer planning more intensive uses. Future plans include a 1.26 million-square-foot regional shopping mall, hotels, commercial/office buildings, retail establishments, and multifamily housing: in total, more than 14 million square feet of development.

SPECIFIC PROGRAM CHARACTERISTICS

Denton County Road Utility District No. 1

In recognition of the need for infrastructure to support anticipated development, landowners in the area petitioned the State Highway and Public Transportation Commission to create the Denton County Road Utility District (RUD) No.1 to finance the needed road improvements. The Denton RUD No.1 was created in 1986 and confirmed at an election held within the district (in which the vote was one in favor, none against).

The district is composed of 1,344 acres primarily within Denton County with approximately 62 acres in Dallas County; it is entirely within the City of Lewisville which annexed the territory in November 1984. It was formed to finance, purchase, and construct road and drainage facilities. More specifically, improvements include construction and/or improvement of 7.4 miles of arterial and main feeder routes, construction of a highway interchange, and installation of storm drainage.

The district has no full-time employees nor are any planned for the future since, once completed, the facilities will be conveyed to the State Department of Highways and the City of Lewisville for future maintenance and administration. Until the facilities are given to the state, the district is administered by the board of governors, selected and approved by the landowners within the district.

In 1986, market valuation of property in the Denton RUD was slightly over $35 million. The road district floated $8.1 million of bonds in 1987, equal to 23 percent of taxable assessed valuation, and about a $6,000 debt per acre. An initial (1987) tax rate was proposed of $0.43 per $100 of property valuation; given an average debt service of over $789,000, this rate would have to jump six fold unless property values rise significantly. However, preliminary estimates indicate the assessed value has more than doubled, largely because these properties are no longer classified as agricultural land. Extensive development is planned for the district, with three more bond issues scheduled for the next three years, each roughly the size of the original issue.

In addition to taxes assessed by the RUD, some property will be assessed taxes by the Denton County Levee Improvement District No. 1 to pay for debt service on $4.4 million of bonds being floated for a levee and retention system to provide adequate drainage in the area. Additional debt issued by the two school districts operating within the road district, the counties, and the City of Lewisville bring gross debt (direct and overlapping) to 40 percent of 1986 taxable assessed district valuation.

At the present time, there are only three significant taxpayers within the Denton RUD. The significant growth of the district's tax base (and hence ease with which debt can be repaid) is directly related to future district development, primarily industrial and commercial. However, formation of the RUD does not obligate the property owners to begin or continue development of their land. Development plans include over 400 acres of multifamily residential units, nearly 580 acres of light industry, and approximately 170 acres of general business including a 100-acre major regional shopping center.

Northwest Travis County Road District No. 2

The Northwest Travis CRD is located in the northwestern part of the county, entirely within the Austin city limits. It is composed of approximately 59 acres of bare land (but with all utilities on site and roads under construction) at the intersection of U.S. Highway 183 and a farm to market road; it is approximately 7 miles north of the central business district. The district was established by order of the county commissioners' court in February 11, 1986. On the same day, a petition signed by more than half of the district's qualified voters was presented to the court requesting an election to determine whether or not bonds would be issued. An April election was held, and the lone vote cast endorsed bond issues up to an aggregate of $4.5 million.

Although the Texas constitution allows road district debt to reach 25 percent of net assessed valuation of taxable real property, the Travis County Commissioners' Court set a lower limit of 20 percent. The 1987 bond issue for $3.5 million constitutes a debt burden of 18.48 percent of the 1986 net taxable assessed valuation and constitutes $91,575 in funded debt per taxable acre. (The district includes 20.7 acres in non-taxable land, mostly rights-of-way for the planned improvements.)

Improvements estimated to cost $4.55 million are scheduled for the district, $2.43 million funded from proceeds of the 1987 bond issue. The balance of the revenue received from the $3.5 million bond sale is allocated to capitalized interest, underwriter's discount, and other costs of issuance such as legal fees. The balance of road improvement costs will be financed by the interested developer and predominant landowner, or through future bond issues. Annual debt service for the 1987 bond issue ranges from a first-year low of $138,411 to a high of $462,062 and averages $419,434. Assuming a 90 percent collection rate, a tax rate of $2.461 per $100 of 1986 net taxable assessed valuation is required to support the average debt service.

Southwest Williamson County Road District No. 1

This CRD was established by the commissioners' court in September 1985 in response to a petition by a majority of the qualified voters in the proposed district; the court ordered a public hearing and, subsequently, an election. At a November 1985 election, two thirds of the voters approved the issuance of an aggregate of $81.5 million of unlimited tax road bonds for road construction and improvements. The Williamson CRD borders the northwestern limits of Austin, and a small portion of the district lies within the city limits; it contains approximately 2,352 acres, surrounding the intersection of U.S. Highway 183 and Farm to Market Road 620. Historically, the area has been devoted primarily to low-density uses such as agriculture and ranching. Expenditures and related bond issues are scheduled over the next 15 years in three planned phases to coincide with development anticipated in the district. Phase A, slated for completion by January 1988, consists of construction of a loop road, a portion of an east-west minor arterial, and the central collector road, plus the signalization and channelization of certain key intersections. Phase B, to be completed by January 1992, would extend the loop road and other roads built in Phase A, plus a highway interchange. Phase C, with completion anticipated by 2000, would include various crossovers designed by the district but, if possible, constructed by the state highway department.

As of January 1, 1986, net taxable assessed value of properties in the district totalled $102.8 million distributed among 14 taxpaying landowners holding approximately 1,474 acres. Property accounting for 47 percent of the assessed value (but only 16 percent of the land area) was held by only two landowners. In addition, the State of Texas owns 772 acres of tax-exempt district land, currently mandated by the state legislature to be sold to private entities.

With the sale of the second bond issue in November 1986, these landowners became responsible for district debt of $25 million, a debt burden equal to 23.4 percent of net taxable assessed valuation or $10,333 of funded debt per acre. Overlapping debt, issued by the cities of Austin and Cedar Park and the school district constitute an additional burden equal to 3.3 percent of assessed valuation.

Average annual debt service requirements of the two district bond issues floated so far amount to $2.746 million, requiring a tax rate of $2.98 per $100 of 1986 net taxable assessed valuation (assuming a 90 percent collection rate). Assessed valuation in 1986 ranged from below $300/acre for property under agricultural use exemption to $198,379/acre for property with high-density zoning; if the anticipated development of the properties and significant increases in assessed values are realized in the future, the tax rate will drop substantially.

EXPERIENCE

The bond issues to finance the three road districts were floated in late 1986 and early 1987, so it is too soon to assess progress.

APPLICABILITY

The nature of Texas RUDs and CRDs is similar to special assessment improvement districts elsewhere. They differ in several respects, most importantly in the use of ad valorem taxes rather than fees based on a property's physical characteristics. Since ad valorem fees are comparable to general property taxes, some jurisdictions may require special legislation to create similar districts. In fact, most other special districts have not levied fees based on property values, and many prefer to avoid any such assessment. For example, although ad valorem assessments are allowed under California law, many believe that these would be too close in nature to property taxes which are limited by Proposition 13 and would, in any case, provoke taxpayer resistance. Recently, Texas enacted legislation that broadened the allowable fee basis for CRDs and RUDs to include fees based on factors other than assessed property value. (These factors were not specified in the legislation; determination of the basis for assessment was left to district boards and constraints on allowable factors have not yet been legally defined.)

In the Denver Mall District described below, assessments are based on land area rather than property value. Because assessments were based on non-fluctuating bases in the Denver, Pleasanton, and Montana cases, the amount of the fees were stated in advance for each bond issue, and the proportion of revenue from any single landowner was fixed at that time. In the case of the Denton RUD, however, only an initial tax rate could be specified; subsequent rates will be determined in accordance with fluctuations in assessed valuation of district property. No initial rates were specified in the prospectuses for the two CRDs considered here.

The use of ad valorem special assessments rather than predetermined assessments based on physical measures means that the tax level and proportion of the tax burden borne by any single landowner will shift over time if development is uneven within the district. These shifts do not appear to have created major problems. In Texas road districts, annual revenue from the special taxes must meet debt service incurred for road improvements and, therefore, property tax rates are set to yield a target revenue given the assessed tax valuation of all properties within the special district. Thus, the special taxes assessed against one property are directly related not only to the level of development of that property but also to the level of development of all other properties within the district.

Nonetheless, if development proceeded more slowly than planned, a greater than anticipated tax burden could be imposed on the few landowners whose property had been developed first. In extreme cases, particularly if concurrent with economic recession, individual landowners may go bankrupt, thus placing an even greater burden on remaining landowners and perhaps precipitating further insolvencies. This is a variation of the general risks of development-based financing noted above in the introduction to this chapter.

In fact, interest in special districts has increased in the Austin area. Owners whose property is developed early expect to pay a higher share of the total burden because they benefit most immediately from the improvements. Those who develop later defer their tax burden but they also defer any return on their investment through sale of developed properties.

REFERENCES

Denton County Road District No. 1:

Barry Pound (Chairman, Board of Directors of the Denton RUD)
Barta and Pound Public Relations
8435 Stemmons Freeway
Suite 144
Dallas, Texas 75247
Phone (214) 631-3200

Northwest Travis County Road District No. 2:

Don Bosse (Project Coordinator)
Director of Land Development
Hughes Interests
515 Congress Avenue
Suite 1800
Austin, Texas 78701
Phone (512) 499-8200

Southwest Williamson County Road District No. l:

Michael Reinhardt
LandBank
1301 Capital of Texas Highway South
Building A, Suite 300
Austin, Texas 78746
Phone (512) 327-9470

DAVENPORT, IOWA
TAX INCREMENT FINANCING

SUMMARY

The City of Davenport, Iowa, is using tax increment financing to fund close to $4 million of a $13.2 million road and utilities improvement project in a newly created economic development area. Improvements include four new Interstate highway ramps, two bridges over the highway, and improvements to local roads. Over the next ten years, the city anticipates spending more than $40 million for infrastructure within the development area to facilitate commercial and residential development.

BACKGROUND

Davenport is one of four cities that make up the Quad Cities metropolitan area. Straddling the Mississippi River, this area had a 1987 population of approximately 490,000 distributed among Davenport and Bettendorf, Iowa, and Rock Island and Moline (and East Moline), Illinois. The first Quad Cities area-wide transportation plan was adopted in 1969. This plan called for construction of an additional interchange along the stretch of I-74 that divides Davenport and Bettendorf. These two cities requested an acceleration of plans. The need for such an interchange was reiterated in a study commissioned by a developer proposing to build a regional shopping center in the immediate vicinity. State funds, however, were insufficient for such a project.

Subsequent plans, adopted in 1976 and 1986, reaffirmed the need for the interchange and identified it as the responsibility of the City of Davenport. This interchange is just one portion of plans for improved roadways in northeast Davenport and northern Bettendorf. These improvements have been justified on the grounds that traffic volumes exceed capacity on several roadways and, probably more importantly, on the grounds that such improvements would facilitate the commercial and residential development planned for the area. (Current land use in the area is indicated on the accompanying map.) State Department of Transportation (DOT) funds were not available either, because they were shifted almost entirely to preserve the existing road system, leaving little for such new projects.

The City of Davenport has been involved directly in economic development since 1978 through its Community Development Department. The department uses various inducements to attract new businesses such as favorable zoning, tax abatement, industrial development revenue bonds, and a revolving loan program. In 1986, the city expanded its development efforts with the creation of two additional economic development areas (EDAs), one of which encompassed the relatively undeveloped area adjacent to the proposed I-74 interchange.

By early 1986, two development companies had expressed interest in the I-74 EDA; in both cases, actual development is contingent upon the construction of the interchange. One company had already spent more than $0.5 million since 1978 to conduct market and land use analyses, complete site and engineering design studies, and construct street

DAVENPORT, IOWA: Existing land use in area of proposed 53rd Street/Interstate 74 interchange.

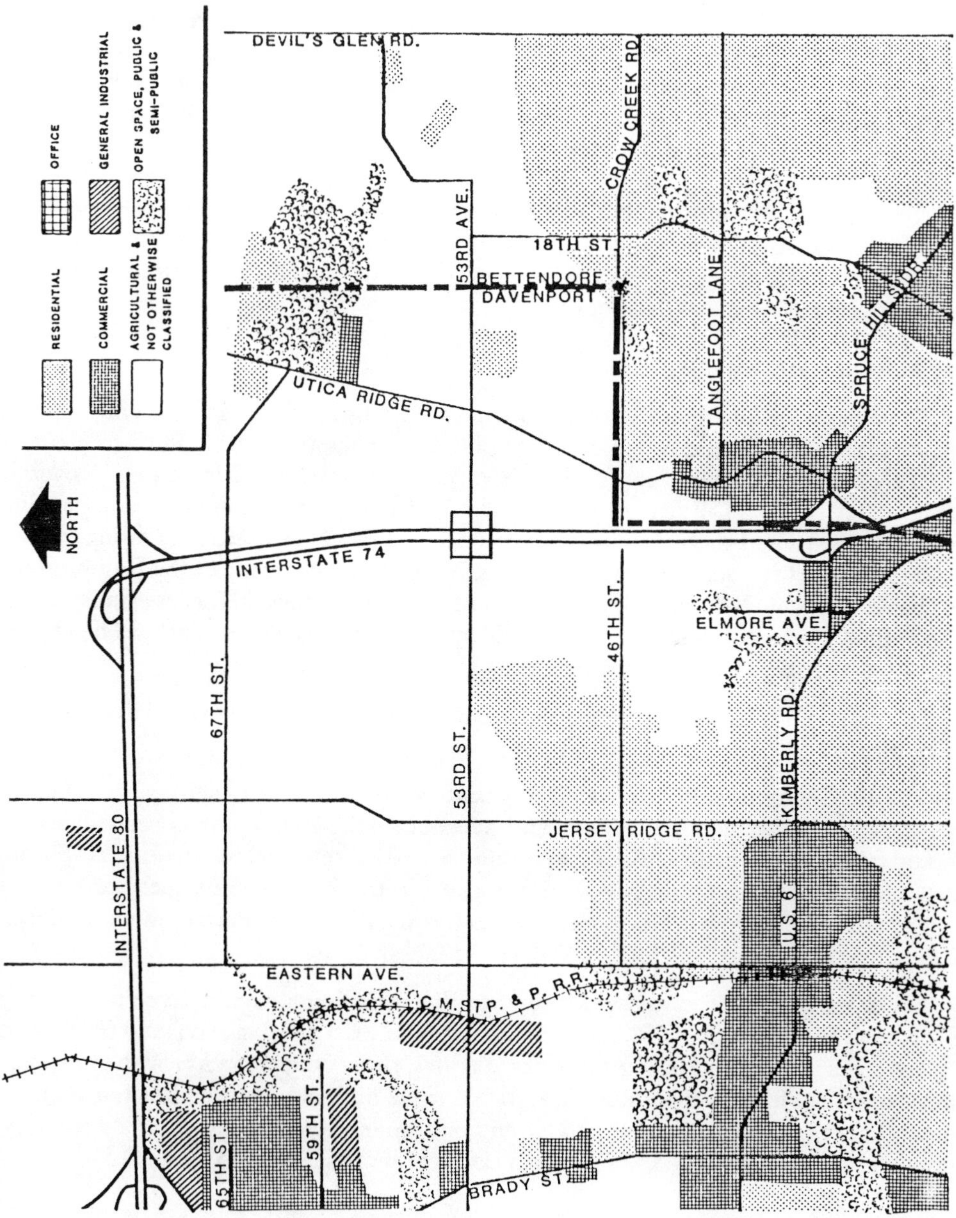

and sewer improvements. Of their 422-acre parcel, nearly 50 acres is targeted for commercial (office and retail) development. Despite this investment, location on this site had been rejected by other firms because of lack of direct access to I-74.

Overall, total capital investment needed to develop the I-74 EDA is estimated at $47 million. Of this total, $8.65 million is in land (1984 assessed value), and over $25 million in buildings. The remaining $13.2 million is public investment in roadway and utility improvements needed to induce development. Because state funding was not available for the full cost of these public works, Davenport applied to the RISE (Revitalize Iowa's Sound Economy) Fund for a grant of $2.5 million plus a loan of an additional $2.5 million to be repaid over a period of ten years. Davenport created the I-74 Tax Increment Financing (TIF) District to repay this loan and, in general, to support the financing of the road and utilities needed, including the interchange. In addition to TIF revenues, support for these improvements will come from the proceeds of general obligation bonds, special assessments, and dedications, contributions, and direct charges collected from property owners and developers.

PROGRAM CHARACTERISTICS

The revenue available for investment from a TIF district is the increase in property tax receipts over a pre-development base level of receipts--that is, the increment in property taxes attributable to development (net of inflation and increases in overall property tax rates). TIF revenues from the I-74 District (shown in the accompanying map) will be applied via two routes to provide a portion of the funds facilitating the full commercial and residential development of the land in the vicinity of the proposed interchange. First, half of the TIF revenues collected are earmarked for repayment of the $2.5 million loan from the RISE Fund; principal and interest (2 percent) will be repaid over a ten-year period, beginning two years after project completion.

Second, the remaining TIF revenues are to be applied directly to the infrastructure investments.

The RISE Fund, supported with a 2-cent-per-gallon motor fuel tax, is a special economic development highway fund and is flexible in the loan repayment schedules accepted from local jurisdictions. Thus, rather than being required to repay its RISE fund loan in equal annual installments, Davenport will repay it as TIF revenues accrue, that is, payments will be low in the initial years and rise with time as development proceeds in the targeted area.

For the defined TIF district, Davenport officials anticipate an increase in property assessment valuations from $8.6 million in 1984 to at least $21.3 million, and possibly as high as $59.2 million, by 1994. At current tax rates, this would mean a growth in property tax revenues from a 1984 base of $280,000 to $2 million or more after ten years of development -- a tax increment of $1.7 million a year. Even the low estimate for 1994 property tax revenues ($725,435) yields a tax increment of $445,435 annually.

DAVENPORT, IOWA: Proposed Tax Increment Financing District

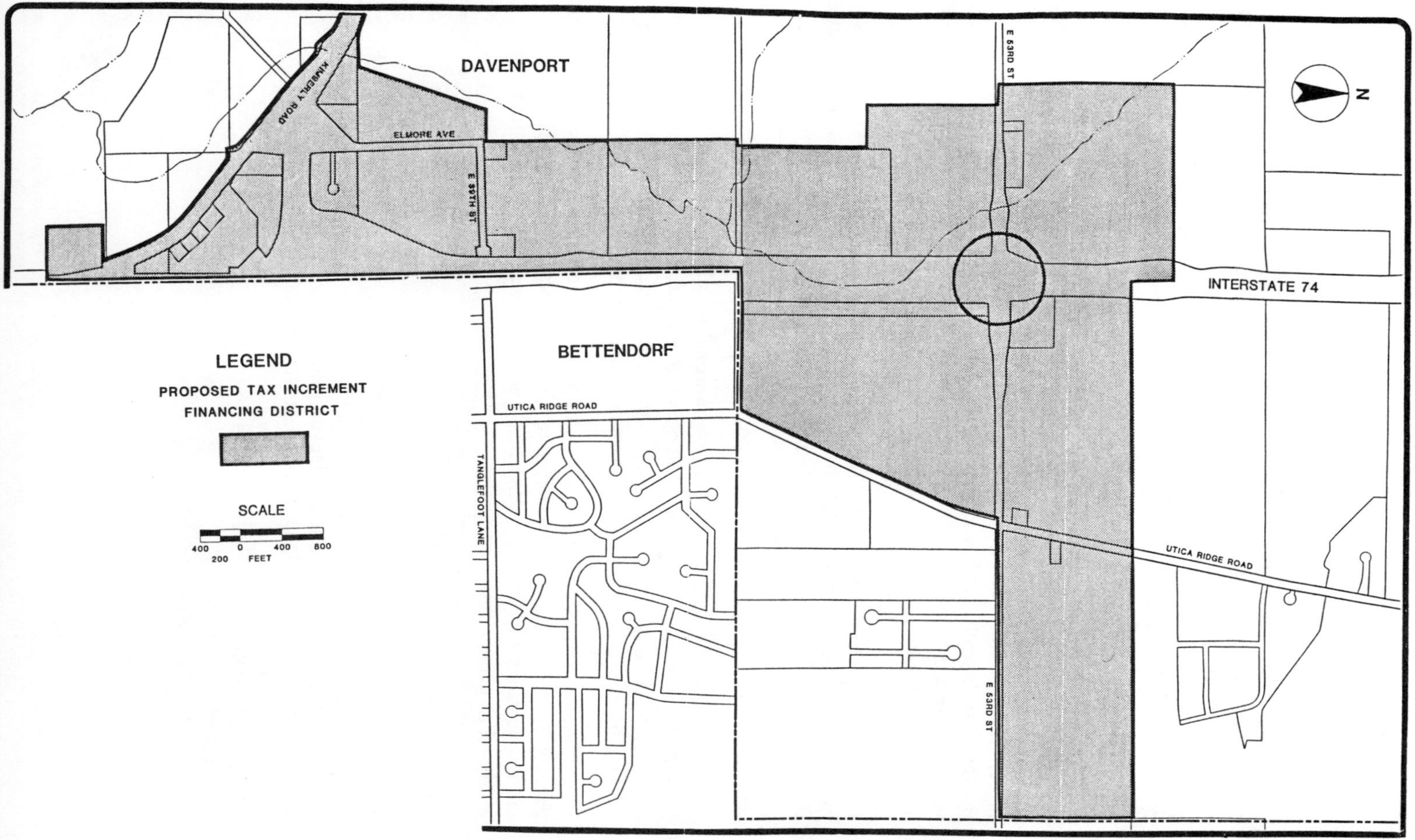

EXPERIENCE

By early 1987, approximately $700,000 had been spent on engineering and feasibility studies. Construction of the I-74 interchange is expected to begin in spring 1987 and to be completed by summer-fall 1989 at the earliest. Because the project has only just begun, TIF revenues have not yet been realized. However, the city is now rezoning the land from agricultural to commercial property, and it is anticipated that this in itself will increase property values. Several companies have already expressed an interest in developments in the TIF district; one plans a major hotel.

APPLICABILITY

Tax increment financing districts have been used in other jurisdictions to fund improvements that, in turn, promote the rise in property values and taxes underwriting these improvements. TIF districts are feasible for all types of infrastructure built within the defined district and have the advantage that, because no additional taxes are assessed, there are no market distortions introduced (see Chapter II discussion on market sensitivity). Clearly, only infrastructure that promotes development or otherwise increases property values is justified when using TIF funding; this makes such financing more limited in applicability than special assessment districts. In Davenport's case, the availability of capital from the RISE Fund and a liberal repayment schedule facilitated the project. In other areas, TIF revenues have been used to support bond issues where the risk is borne by private bondholders rather than the state. In these cases, the burden of higher, market-level, interest payments must be added to project costs.

The potential disadvantages of programs such as Davenport's are those associated with all development-dependent financing, discussed above in the introduction to this chapter. Additional problems of public perception are noted in the applicability section of the next case study on Prince George's County, Maryland.

Although the 1986 Tax Reform Act imposes a stricter limit on the proportion of tax-exempt bond revenues used to support private purposes, this restriction has no practical implications for Iowa TIF districts since, in Iowa, TIF district financing is legally confined to wholly public projects.

REFERENCES

Davenport:

Michael Wilson
Associate Director for Economic Development
Community and Economic Development Department
City of Davenport,
226 W. Fourth Street
Davenport, Iowa 52801
Phone (319) 326-7766

RISE Fund:

Gunnar Rorbakken
Transportation Planner
Iowa Department of Transportation
800 Lincoln Way
Ames, Iowa 50010
Phone (515) 239-1315

PRINCE GEORGE'S COUNTY, MARYLAND TAX INCREMENT FINANCING

SUMMARY

Because of a 1978 tax limit initiative that froze regular property tax revenues, Prince George's County needed another source of funds for capital financing. However, the state legislature specified that funds raised through tax increment financing (TIF) in specially created districts were not subject to limits imposed by such initiatives. The county utilized this exemption and created a number of special districts in which expected increments in property tax revenues were used to support bond issues for infrastructure investment.

BACKGROUND

Prince George's County is a 487-square-mile area to the east of Washington, D.C., with a moderate-income population of more than 500,000. In early 1983, only 38 percent of this land was developed; of this, 60 percent was in residential and 10 percent in commercial and industrial uses. It is currently enjoying a surge in development and was second among the Washington, D.C., jurisdictions in new commercial construction with 4 million square feet built in 1985.

In 1978, voters in Prince George's County endorsed the Tax Reform Initiative by Marylanders (TRIM) amendment through a referendum. Similar to other cases of taxpayer initiative, TRIM limited general property tax revenues. In contrast to Proposition 13 in California, which put a ceiling on the millage tax rate, the TRIM amendment placed an absolute ceiling on property tax revenues of $143.9 million per year with no adjustments for inflation or growth. Inflation, therefore, eroded the real (constant dollar) value of revenues, causing many cutbacks in capital improvement programs.

Although an integral part of the Washington, D.C., metropolitan area, the county had not captured its share of the region's new office projects and high-tech industrial development. Moreover, most new development in the county had been occurring outside its urbanized areas and increasingly further away from the metropolitan core, leading to a pattern of urban sprawl. The desire to attract and manage new commercial and industrial development combined with the financial constraints imposed by TRIM forced Prince George's County public officials to search for new financing mechanisms.

Tax increment financing (TIF) had already been discussed both within the Maryland State Department of Economic and Community Development and with county officials and members of the Chamber of Commerce as early as 1977. In July 1980, the state legislature passed the Maryland Tax Increment Finance Act. With the constraints imposed by the 1978 passage of TRIM and the state legislature's stipulation that funds raised through TIF districts were not subject to local budget caps such as TRIM, implementation of tax increment financing seemed a logical source of capital funds for Prince George's County.

PROGRAM CHARACTERISTICS

In Maryland, TIF districts are limited by law to 10 percent of the land area. Originally designed to generate revenues to repay bonds, the legislature amended the act to allow TIF districts to be created in anticipation of development and without concomitant bond issuance. Thus, once TIF districts are established, the designated TIF income may be accumulated in TIF district funds for future public investments on a bonded or pay-as-you-go basis. When bonds are issued, the total TIF debt service is limited to 15 percent of total county debt service.

TIF districts in Prince George's County were designed to underwrite transportation projects in areas suitable for industrial and commercial development. Impetus for creating a district can come from the public or the private sector; proposals are submitted to the county executive for recommendation to the county council which gives the final approval. The areas selected for creation of districts have been chosen to a greater or lesser degree because of their growth potential and in coordination with the total economic development program. For example, four districts contain an existing or proposed Metro subway station.

Investment projects are expected to be either part of or at least consistent with approved county plans for development, land use, public facilities, and capital improvements; this is to ensure that expenditures benefit county development and are not just improvements sought by developers attempting to shift costs to the county. Within each district, priorities are set in the same manner as for non-TIF capital projects, with highest priorities addressed first and those of lower priority undertaken as growth generates additional TIF revenues.

For each new district, the county assessment office surveys the area to determine the base value for all properties within the district. All taxes from this base continue to be allocated to the general fund; the incremental revenues are allocated to the TIF district fund and continue to accumulate until projects are undertaken.

According to Janet Everette in the Prince George's County Office of Management and Budget, bonds issued to fund TIF projects in the county were either general obligation (GO) bonds or Maryland Department of Transportation bonds rather than revenue bonds supported only by TIF revenues. Thus, although TIF revenues were administratively earmarked for debt service, legally pledged financial support was not confined to them. This is in contrast to other examples such as Orlando, Florida, also described in this book.

EXPERIENCE

The first Prince George's County TIF district was created to raise matching funds of $3 to 4 million for an Amtrak station parking garage. The county issued a tax allocation bond to finance the development. Because the bond was to be backed only by the TIF revenues and was not a GO bond, the interest rate was higher than the already high rates for county GO bonds. The high cost led the county to withdraw the bond and wait for a later reissue at lower rates. Bonds were reissued in 1983 and 1984.

A second district was created in response to a 40-acre office park development requiring rezoning and highway improvements. The developer could not afford the $1.2 million road improvements and the town opposed the development without road improvements, and extensions. The developer initiated TIF district considerations, and the district was established in 1981 with improvements planned for 1983.

As of January 1986, ten districts had been created in the county. The total taxable base of these districts exceeded $500 million with $200 million representing the original assessment base and the remainder derived from growth.

In fiscal year 1985, TIF revenues were $4.68 million of which approximately $2.0 million was expended on debt service, $0.4 on capital projects directly, and nearly all of the balance was reserved for district purposes. In the 1987 fiscal year budget, TIF revenues are estimated to be $8 million with debt service of $2.8 million.

In November 1984, Prince George's County voters passed the Fairness for All County Taxpayers (FACT) referendum which modified the TRIM restrictions so that the absolute tax revenue ceiling of $143.9 million was rescinded and replaced with a tax **rate** ceiling. The FACT referendum also freed all assessable base revenues including TIF revenues to go into the general fund. This was in line with criticism of the county administration for maintaining a surplus in the TIF funds when revenues were needed outside the districts.

Thus, with reserves accumulated from past years plus the excess over debt service needs in 1987, it is anticipated that $16.7 million of TIF-based revenues will be transferred to the County General Fund. As a corollary of this action, major projects previously targeted for TIF funding were included in a $82 million transportation program passed in a November, 1986 referendum. By fiscal 1988, all tax revenues collected in TIF districts will be allocated to the general fund except those necessary for debt service on TIF-based projects.

Based on their experience, Prince George's County officials caution jurisdictions against creating TIF districts that do not follow traditional election or assessment district boundaries because of difficulties in establishing a data base and administering a uniquely defined district. They advise officials to work closely with the area assessor's office in delineating the districts.

APPLICABILITY

Clearly, Prince George's County officials, when legally and financially permitted to do so, prefer to work through the general fund and issue GO bonds to finance infrastructure projects. In this, as well as its longer experience with TIF districts, Prince George's County differs from Davenport. Nonetheless, Prince George's County officials note that using a TIF process has some advantages: tax allocation bonds backed by TIF revenues can be issued more quickly than GO bonds which require voter approval. Tax increment financing also gives the county a pro-development image.

County officials also note that a TIF program can have some disadvantages: there may be a public misperception that TIF districts get public improvements when other areas do not; that TIF funds may be inadequate to recapture public investment or support planned improvements; that unless well-defined programs are delineated, developers may also perceive of the program as uneven and unfair; that developers in a TIF district feel the TIF funds generated are "their" money. Moreover, sometimes property owners in TIF districts think they are paying a higher tax rate than elsewhere even though their rate is the same as in the rest of the jurisdiction and the special TIF funds are generated by a diversion of receipts from general revenue to earmarked projects.

The constraints imposed by the 1986 Tax Reform Act would probably not affect replication of the Prince George's County program since the funds were used for public works projects.

REFERENCE

James R. Novak
Director
Public Works and Transportation
Prince George's County
County Administration Building
Upper Marlboro, Maryland, 20772
Phone (301) 952-4150

MISSOULA, MONTANA
RURAL SPECIAL IMPROVEMENT DISTRICTS

SUMMARY

This example is included because while Missoula is a slow-growing rural area, with low population density, it has been successful in applying special improvement districts, a technique usually associated with places of higher density.

BACKGROUND

After rapid growth during the 1970s, Missoula County has remained stable in the 1980s. Current population totals approximately 77,300. The county has been using the rural special improvement district (RSID) program to finance a variety of infrastructure projects since 1965, including investments in roads, utility extensions, sewer plants, and water projects. In addition to RSIDs for infrastructure expansion, Missoula also uses perpetual maintenance RSIDs (that is, created for infrastructure maintenance without time limits) to support upkeep of improvements installed under the program.

PROGRAM CHARACTERISTICS

Two categories of RSID are defined by the Missoula County Board of Commissioners: neighborhood and developer RSIDs. **Neighborhood RSIDs** are created primarily to improve the quality of life and surroundings for residents already in the district and do not necessarily involve land speculation or bringing the land to marketable standards. Although the board may create RSIDs on its own volition, petitions from neighborhood residents have been required as a matter of policy unless public health and safety are involved. Petitions require approval by 60 percent of the freeholders in the proposed district.

Developer RSIDs are created when, in the proposed district, 51 percent of the land area is owned by a single person, partnership, or corporation intending to improve this land to a marketable condition. Alternately, a developer RSID may be created even if a single entity does not hold 51 percent of the land but will be responsible for at least 40 percent of the cost of the contemplated improvements.

Creation of both neighborhood and developer RSIDs can be nullified by protest from owners of property responsible for more than 50 percent of the cost of the proposed work. However, protests against RSIDs for sanitary sewers may be overruled by unanimous vote of the board.

Allocation of improvement costs among the landholders for both types of RSIDs is at the option of the county board of commissioners and can be according to:

- Proportion of assessable area (which may be less than total lot area in the district);
- Proportion of assessed value;

- Proportion of lineal feet abutting a street; or
- For utility connections, a lump sum per connection.

EXPERIENCE

Since the program's inception in 1965, almost 900 RSIDs have been created in Missoula County. The full value of individual projects partially or fully funded through RSIDs has ranged from $50,000 to over $1.6 million; projects have involved lighting, curbs and sidewalks, streets, utility infrastructure, and even fire hydrants.

The largest project to date, and one of the most recent, involves extension of a sewer line. The proposed extension, with an estimated total project cost of more than $1.6 million, will be funded in large part (55 percent) by a federal grant from the Environmental Protection Agency. The balance will be provided by Missoula County and Missoula City Aid-to-Construction grants, a City of Missoula loan, funds from city connection fees of $350 per unit, and RSID funds of $289,000. The RSID funds, in turn, will be collected from two sources: a local development company that is building 2,625 housing units and that created an RSID for $140,000 (this represents the 48 percent of future loading required by the new development); and $150,000 from 285 initial participating residences (outside the development company's RSID) organized in one or several RSIDs. Future connections in the area will have to pay equivalent amounts per unit as an RSID rebate to be divided evenly between retirement of bonds floated for the project and the city's loan. When the bonds have been retired, the city will receive all rebates.

APPLICABILITY

Missoula's experience demonstrates better than other single case studies the wide range of infrastructure investments for which special assessment district financing is appropriate; it also differs from other case studies in the use of special assessment district financing in established residential neighborhoods and in areas of low population density. In this county, projects range from maintenance of infrastructure in existing neighborhoods to installation of new infrastructure in both developed and undeveloped areas. The advantages and disadvantages associated with Missoula's special districts are those associated with all special assessment districts and are discussed in Chapter II and the introduction to Chapter III.

REFERENCE

John DeVore
Operations Officer
Department of General Services
Missoula County Courthouse Annex
Missoula, Montana 59802
Phone (406) 721-5700, extension 391

FORT COLLINS, COLORADO SPECIAL IMPROVEMENT DISTRICTS

SUMMARY

Fort Collins uses special improvement districts (SIDs) to finance infrastructure development supported by special assessments levied against the property owners in each defined district. Fort Collins distinguishes two categories of district: involuntary SIDs and voluntary SIDs. Voluntary SIDs differ from most special districts because participation is not mandatory for all landowners.

BACKGROUND

The City of Fort Collins is located at the eastern base of the "Front Range" of the Rocky Mountains, 65 miles north of Denver, and serves as a regional trade center for northern Colorado, southern Wyoming, and western Nebraska. Originally an agricultural community, Fort Collins has attracted a growing number of national electronics firms. In 1985, population was slightly over 82,000, up 46 percent from 1975. Of the population over 25 years old, 36 percent had college degrees. Colorado State University is the single largest employer with close to 6,500 employees.

In the financing and support of its public works, the City of Fort Collins adheres to the principle of user funding--that is, a close relationship between payments made and benefits received. Two approaches were taken, both of which link payments and benefits and insulate public works from the uncertainties of the general budgetary allocation process. First, Fort Collins created individual utilities to manage water, sewer, stormwater, and transportation. Second, in undeveloped areas, Fort Collins created special improvement districts, using special assessments collected from each property owner to fund the infrastructure that will benefit them directly. (A description of Fort Collins' utilities is presented in Chapter V.) In both instances, therefore, costs are borne by the beneficiaries. In both cases, also, public works finances and planning are independent of fiscal limitations associated with the general revenue budget.

PROGRAM CHARACTERISTICS

Under the Fort Collins program, two types of special improvement districts are recognized: voluntary and involuntary. **Involuntary SIDs** are generally initiated by the city when the administration recognizes the need for infrastructure investments in a given geographical area. If 51 percent of the property owners approve its creation, the SID is formed and all landowners are required to pay the fees assessed to support the proposed improvements. The forced inclusion of any dissenters makes the Fort Collins involuntary SIDs similar to the special districts in Missoula, Montana, and Pleasanton, California.

Voluntary SIDs are formed by petition of a group of property owners in a given area. The petition process is similar to that in Missoula and Pleasanton but with an important difference: landowners who do not choose to join the SID cannot be forced to pay their fair share of the costs even if a preponderance of landowners want to form a SID and even if the holdout(s) will benefit from the proposed improvements. SIDs may be formed by any group of petitioners who agree to underwrite all the infrastructure costs themselves, at least initially. They may negotiate with the holdout(s) for subsequent reimbursement. These inter-landowner agreements can be incorporated in legal contracts, the specific arrangements of which are up to the individual property owners and the SID members.

EXPERIENCE

Historically, these districts have been created in undeveloped areas requiring new or improved public works prior to further economic development, though the mechanism could be equally well applied to districts created in established areas.

APPLICABILITY

The special improvement districts in Fort Collins are similar to other special assessment districts described in this book; the unique element is the noncompulsory membership and introduction of intra-district bargaining in the voluntary SIDs. This feature may be particularly attractive for jurisdictions in which there appears to be strong opposition to special assessments by individuals within potential district boundaries. If strong opposition precludes creation of more conventional special assessment districts, the use of districts with voluntary membership and intra-district bargaining may facilitate district formation and the initiation of needed infrastructure investments.

REFERENCE

Matt Baker
Special Improvement District Coordinator
City of Fort Collins
P.O. Box 580
Fort Collins, Colorado 80522
Phone (303) 221-6700

EVANSTON, WYOMING SPECIAL ASSESSMENT DISTRICT

SUMMARY

The City of Evanston, Wyoming created a special assessment district to support a 1985 bond financing of land acquisition and infrastructure improvements in the downtown area. This is a good example of the use of special districts by a small city.

BACKGROUND

Evanston is located in the extreme southwestern corner of Wyoming, 83 miles northeast of Salt Lake City, Utah. Population was approximately 11,120 in 1984, an increase of 4,700 since 1980. The city accounts for about half of the total population of Uinta County. The local economy has been affected by the recent development of oil and gas reserves in the Overthrust Belt, currently being explored and developed by several major oil companies. The county has three gas processing plants in operation and one more under construction. Of the county's agricultural land, 90 percent is devoted to livestock though, since 1975, the number of cattle appears to have declined. Because Evanston is the county seat and a trade center for the area, a significant number of persons are employed in retail trade and, to a lesser degree, in county, city, and school district administration.

The city designed a plan to improve the downtown area which included construction of a new post office building, new parking areas, and improvements to the road, water, and storm sewer systems. The relocation of the post office from the periphery of town and the other proposed improvements were intended to attract more business activity to the central downtown area. The total cost of the project was estimated at $1,495,000. Of this, about one half was provided by the City of Evanston and the Wyoming Farm Loan Board. The remaining portion was funded through a tax-exempt bond issued in 1985, with repayment from special assessments levied against properties that benefit from the proposed improvements.

PROGRAM CHARACTERISTICS

The city created the Downtown Improvement District composed of the City of Evanston (46 percent), Uinta County (11 percent), and local businesses (43 percent) covering a specified tract of land in Evanston. A tax-exempt serial bond issue was floated in 1985 for $760,000. These bonds do not constitute a debt of either the City of Evanston or Uinta County but are supported by special assessments levied against the members of the Downtown Improvement District in proportion to their land ownership. These assessments are payable in 15 approximately equal annual installments. The exact amount of each annual payment is calculated according to the debt service (interest plus redemption) due in the following year.

The owner of any lot assessed within the district may choose to prepay the assessment at any time; the prepayment must include only the remaining assessment balance plus interest due on the next regular payment date. Residential properties within the district are excluded from assessment until they are converted to commercial use.

Because it was felt that properties closest to the proposed improvements would benefit the most from such investments, properties within the district were grouped into three groups or tiers according to distance from improvements with a different assessment rate for each tier. Thus, properties in Tier 3, farthest from the proposed improvements, were assessed at $0.495 per square foot, properties in Tier 2 at $0.595, and properties in Tier 1 at $0.695 per square foot.

To provide additional security for payment of debt obligations, the city also established a reserve subaccount. Funded with the city's receipts from the state gasoline and cigarette license taxes, this reserve must equal at least 2 percent of the original amount of the bonds issued for a period of ten years.

EXPERIENCE

Using receipts from the bond issue, the City of Evanston bought out businesses on the block slated to become the post office, demolished them, and sold the land to the postal system for construction of the new building. The remainder of the improvements -- purchase of several old houses and conversion of the land to parking areas, investment in road improvements and street lighting -- have all been completed.

APPLICABILITY

The use of special assessment districts is described in this book for other areas (Pleasanton, California, and Missoula, Montana, for example). Clearly, such districts can be used anywhere there is sufficient consensus among landholders willing to fund improvements that benefit their properties. Evanston and Missoula, however, differ from Pleasanton in the considerably smaller size of the assessments involved. Moreover, the Evanston district and most of the districts in Missoula were created to add improvements to land already in use as established commercial or residential areas. In contrast, the last (and most extensive) Missoula district and all the Pleasanton assessment districts involve land being readied for future development either for private residences or commercial/industrial parks. The formation of the assessment district and the criteria for assessment, however, are much the same, demonstrating the fairly general applicability of such an approach when local landowners reach a consensus.

Similar to special assessment districts in Pleasanton, California (discussed above), and Denver, Colorado (presented next), the Evanston district delineated separate zones of benefit and assessment levels geared to levels of benefit assumed to vary with distance from the infrastructure constructed. Such differentiation allows a closer link between financial burden and presumed benefit but, as benefit is difficult to measure, there can be problems of equity in setting the varying assessment levels.

REFERENCE

Albert Hays
Treasurer
City of Evanston
1200 Main Street
Evanston, Wyoming 82930
Phone (307) 789-9690

DENVER, COLORADO BENEFIT ASSESSMENT DISTRICT

SUMMARY

Denver created a special assessment district to support the operation and maintenance costs of a newly constructed transit and shopping mall in the downtown business district. Within the district, assessments are levied against each property owner in accordance with the benefits they are presumed to receive from the mall. Benefits are assumed to vary with distance from the mall and land area of each property.

BACKGROUND

Since the 1890s, Denver's 16th Street has been an important shopping corridor in the Rocky Mountain area. But, in the 1960s, competition from rapidly expanding suburban malls began to have an increasingly harmful effect on downtown shopping. By 1970, the downtown area, though probably still more prosperous than many counterparts in other central cities, was suffering a decline in its share of the expanding regional sales. There was deterioration in facades and storefronts, parking was scarce, large diesel buses clogged downtown streets during peak hours, and there were few pedestrian amenities to attract shoppers.

In 1971, the board of directors of a business advocacy group, Downtown Denver, Inc. (DDI), announced its support of a downtown mall to entice shoppers back downtown. At the same time, the Regional Transportation District (RTD) was investigating ways to relieve the massive congestion of buses downtown. With the 1972 federal rejection of a planned rapid transit system, officials at RTD and DDI began to explore other ways to meet their joint objectives.

Discussion of a downtown mall was revived in 1976 and, in 1977, a plan was presented. This included a mall along 16th Street with bus transfer centers at each end. The central right-of-way was to be dedicated to pedestrian and transit traffic only, with shuttle buses transporting people along the 13-block length of the mall. The plan was well received by most business people as a way to draw people back downtown and revitalize retail activity. An economic benefit study estimated that the new mall would increase sales by at least 7.5 percent.

Mall construction began in early 1980, and the 13-block transit way opened in late 1982. With completion of two transfer stations, all express, intercity, and regional bus routes were revised to end at the two stations rather than traverse the central business district. Total capital costs of the project were $76.1 million, of which $29 million was for mall construction, $5.1 million for the initial 19 shuttle buses, and the remainder to construct the two transfer stations and renovate the RTD administration building. Because the Urban Mass Transportation Administration supported the plan, the project was able to receive approximately 80 percent of the capital costs from the federal government; RTD financed the remaining 20 percent.

Mall supporters realized that construction of the mall was insufficient guarantee of success, and that ongoing promotion and maintenance were also required. These activities, however, were not funded by any federal grants nor were there funds allocated in the RTD budget for such support. As a result, downtown business leaders initiated a 1978 amendment to the city charter to create a special benefit district to finance the care, management, and operation of the mall.

PROGRAM CHARACTERISTICS

The special benefit assessment district created initially was composed only of those properties between 15th and 17th Streets. This included approximately 420 properties and financed a $1.52 million budget for 1983. During this first year of operation, it was increasingly recognized that the district was too small, that benefits extended beyond the boundaries as defined, and that district boundaries ought to be reexamined. A benefit study was commissioned, and the recommendations resulted in the current system.

The benefit study delineated five zones of benefit within an overall district extending between 14th and 19th Streets. This expanded membership to 865 property owners. The accompanying map indicates the location of each zone relative to 16th Street. (The map shows the central portion of the benefit district. The full district extends another half block up and another four blocks down 16th Street.) Zone 1 includes all properties fronting on 16th Street itself--that is, those located between 16th Street and the middle of the block. Zone 2 essentially includes those properties fronting on either side of 17th Street; Zone 3 those fronting on the northeast side of 15th Street and the southwest side of 18th Street; Zone 4 those properties across the street from Zone 3 properties; and Zone 5, properties fronting the northeast side of 14th and the southwest side of 19th Streets. Properties on the far sides of 14th and 19th Streets from the mall are outside the district.

As recommended by the benefit study, assessments vary among zones and, within each zone, are based on square feet of land area rather than land values or square feet of building area. It was felt that assessments based on square footage of land were more straightforward, constant through time, and thus predictable for future years, and that special benefits attributable to the mall have no direct relationship to land value.

Within each of the five zones, those properties in the northwesternmost portion of the assessment district are assessed at half the rate of those on the same streets in the rest of the district. This reflects the lower intensity of development and activity in this area. In effect, this special distinction results in ten zones of benefit based on proximity to 16th Street and intensity of development and activity. Within the district, three nonprofit owners and three low and moderate income-housing projects have been exempted from the special assessments.

Downtown Denver, Inc. (DDI), a nonprofit organization, is responsible for day-to-day management, maintenance, and promotion of the mall under a management agreement with the mall district board. The five-member board is responsible for all policy decisions. The city's manager of public works serves as chairman; the four members represent the downtown community and district property owners. The board is assisted

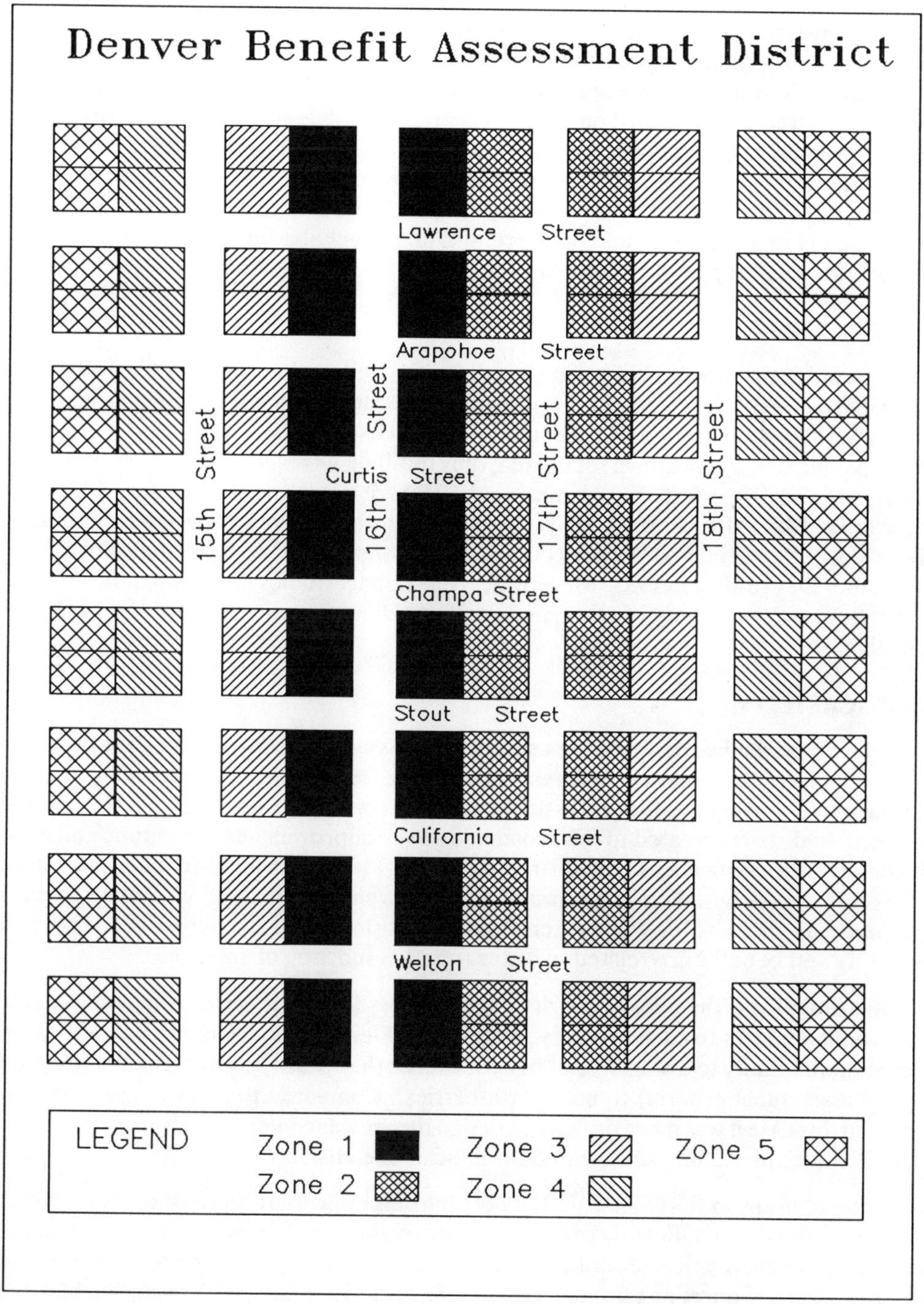
Denver Benefit Assessment District
Lawrence Street
Arapohoe Street
Curtis Street
Champa Street
Stout Street
California Street
Welton Street
15th Street
16th Street
17th Street
18th Street
LEGEND
Zone 1
Zone 2
Zone 3
Zone 4
Zone 5

by advisors from the city council, downtown merchant, development and residential communities, the RTD, Denver police, and The Denver Partnership.

Current assessments range from $0.10 to $0.56 per square foot of land area, depending on zone. These are slightly above those proposed for 1984 which ranged from $0.05 for properties in the northwestern segment of Zone 5 to $0.46 per foot for properties along 16th Street itself. Based on the 1984 proposed budget of $1.68 million, 36 percent of the revenue was from properties at the highest assessment rate and 26 percent from those assessed at the second highest rate. The current budget is estimated as $1.9 million, the bulk of which is paid on a reimbursement basis to The Denver Partnership for management, maintenance, and promotion. The budget also includes funds for capital replacement and repair and a surplus transferred to the capital improvement fund.

EXPERIENCE

Except for the inequities perceived in the initial delineation of the special benefit assessment district (corrected in 1984), the use of special assessments to maintain the 16th Street Mall appears to be well accepted. The mall itself has acted as a catalyst to draw more people to the downtown retail area, thus fulfilling its objectives. In 1984, it was estimated that daily pedestrian volumes were 50,000 or more and that the fare-free shuttle averaged 40,000 passengers a day. Special promotional fairs and events organized by The Denver Partnership draw peak crowds such as the 350,000 or more attending a four-day Labor Day festival in 1985. Moreover, crime impact studies reveal a significant drop in virtually every category of crime in downtown Denver each year since the 1982 mall opening.

APPLICABILITY

Other case studies describe the use of special assessment districts for capital investment. This case is similar in some respects to those, such as Pleasanton, California, and Evanston, Wyoming, in that assessments vary according to proximity to the funded project. In districts created to fund road and sewer improvements which touch on most if not all of the properties in the district such as in Pleasanton and Missoula, allocation of costs is usually based on a measure of the improvements crossing or fronting on each property. In districts for wastewater drainage, storm sewers run across or along each property and benefits are related to water runoff, a function of acreage.

But in Denver, the benefit district could not be defined in terms of physical structures built adjacent to each property. Rather, the Denver mall district boundaries were based on proximity to a single "line" benefit source that yields spin-off benefits (defined by ten assessment criteria) to nearby properties. Compared to other assessment districts, in this case it was more difficult to define the area and intensity of benefits received and therefore more difficult to equitably allocate the costs.

In an attempt to fairly allocate the cost burden in proportion to benefits received, Denver defined a significantly greater number of zones of benefit/assessment than the other assessment districts described. In so doing, however, some problems were created in cases where properties extended beyond the mid-block line dividing zones. In some cases, a single property is assessed at two rates in proportion to the land area in each zone, regardless of the location of the main entrance.

In spite of these problems, the use of benefit assessment districts for financing investment and/or maintenance can be applied to other "line" or "point" structures. For example, properties in the vicinity of a new highway interchange or new transit transfer terminal could be assessed in a similar fashion for initial construction and/or maintenance. To achieve strong support from district property owners, however, it is imperative to define district and zone boundaries so that all beneficiaries are included. Moreover, it is equally important that the basic assessment unit and the variation in assessment per unit are delineated so that landowners feel that assessments are in proportion to perceived benefits.

REFERENCE

Donald F. Turner, Jr.
Director of Operations
The Denver Partnership, Inc.
511 Sixteenth Street
Suite 200
Denver, Colorado 80202-4277
Phone (303) 534-6161

ORLANDO, FLORIDA
TAX INCREMENT FINANCING DISTRICT

SUMMARY

The City of Orlando, Florida, created a community redevelopment trust fund in 1982 to carry out the redevelopment of underdeveloped and less prosperous areas in downtown Orlando. Revenue bonds totalling $19 million were issued to finance the public investments necessary for this project; the increments in property tax revenues expected from redevelopment were pledged to service the debt.

BACKGROUND

The City of Orlando is part of the three-county Orlando Metropolitan Statistical Area (MSA) consisting of Orange, Osceola, and Seminole Counties. The city itself accounted for 143,000, or 17 percent, of the MSA population in 1985. Prior to 1967, the economy of the Orlando MSA was based upon agriculture and citrus products, tourism, light manufacturing, and industries relating to the space program nearby at the Kennedy Space Center. The area had also become a major distribution center for the Florida peninsula.

In the last ten years, Orlando has become home not only to Disney World and other new tourist attractions but also to increasing convention activity. Thus, compared to the nation as a whole, Orlando has a larger than average share of employment in the trade and service sectors. Orlando has also experienced a higher than average growth in high technology industries, more specifically--a growth since 1976 in high-tech employment in Orlando of 114 percent compared to 40 percent nationally. In addition, a number of well-known manufacturing companies have located their headquarters in the Orlando area.

In the period from 1970 to 1985, the MSA population increased by 90 percent to nearly 862,000; a significant portion of this increment was in the prime working age group of 25-44 year-olds. It is projected that by 1990 this age group will have expanded by another 47.5 percent. Total MSA population is anticipated to be over one million by then.

There are two agencies concerned with the economic health of downtown Orlando: the Orlando Downtown Development District Board and the Orlando Community Redevelopment Agency. The Orlando Downtown Development District is composed of approximately 1,000 acres in the heart of downtown Orlando and is governed by a five member board appointed by the mayor for three-year terms. The board has ad valorem taxing powers.

The city council recognized the existence of an area suitable for redevelopment within the larger Downtown Development District. To effect redevelopment of this 569-acre subdistrict, the city council created the City of Orlando Community Redevelopment Agency in February, 1980. The city council then designated itself as the agency responsible for its economic regeneration. The geographical relationship between the downtown development district and the redevelopment subdistrict is shown by the accompanying map.

In 1982, to facilitate the area's redevelopment, the city council adopted a redevelopment plan that outlined a set of programs to be undertaken over ten years and that included upgrading of the aging infrastructure system (water, sewer, etc.), improvement of traffic circulation, creation of additional economic opportunities, additions to the parking system, housing developments, and enhancement of pedestrian environment. The council simultaneously established the Community Redevelopment Trust Fund to collect revenues to support the redevelopment efforts.

PROGRAM CHARACTERISTICS

The redevelopment agency floated several serial revenue bond issues to finance the investments planned for the area. These bonds are not a general obligation of the agency or the City of Orlando. Rather, they are secured by an irrevocable lien on the increment in property tax revenues paid into the trust fund and interest earned by the trust fund. Thus the 569-acre redevelopment district constitutes a tax increment financing (TIF) district. At the time the bonds were issued, private developers had already expressed an interest in the area, and several projects had reached the planning and financing stages.

Several taxing authorities, including the city, the Downtown Development Board, and Orange County, are involved in redevelopment financing within the TIF district. The Library District was also initially included among the participating authorities but is contesting this obligation, and the situation has not yet been resolved.

For each property within its jurisdiction and within the redevelopment area, the taxing authorities pay into the Trust Fund 95 percent of the difference between ad valorem tax revenues actually received and the ad valorem tax revenues that would have been received if the millage rate and assessments had remained at January 1, 1981 levels: that is, 95 percent of the increase in property tax revenues for each taxing authority.

EXPERIENCE

Significant building activity has continued in downtown Orlando with construction of new buildings and renovation of many existing downtown structures. There are expansions in office space (over one million square feet of new office space under construction or planned in the full Downtown Development District), retail space, residential projects, hotels (five major hotels before the end of 1989 including 632 new rooms already opened), and several mixed-use projects (the largest is scheduled for completion by 1995 and includes over one million square feet of office space, 100,000 square feet of retail space, a 200,000 square foot trade mart, and 550 new hotel rooms in two hotels). A 15,000-seat arena, already under construction, is scheduled for completion by January 1989.

The aggregate assessed valuation of taxable real property in the redevelopment area as of January 1, 1981 (the "frozen tax base" of the TIF district) used to determine the

Downtown Development District & Orlando Redevelopment Area

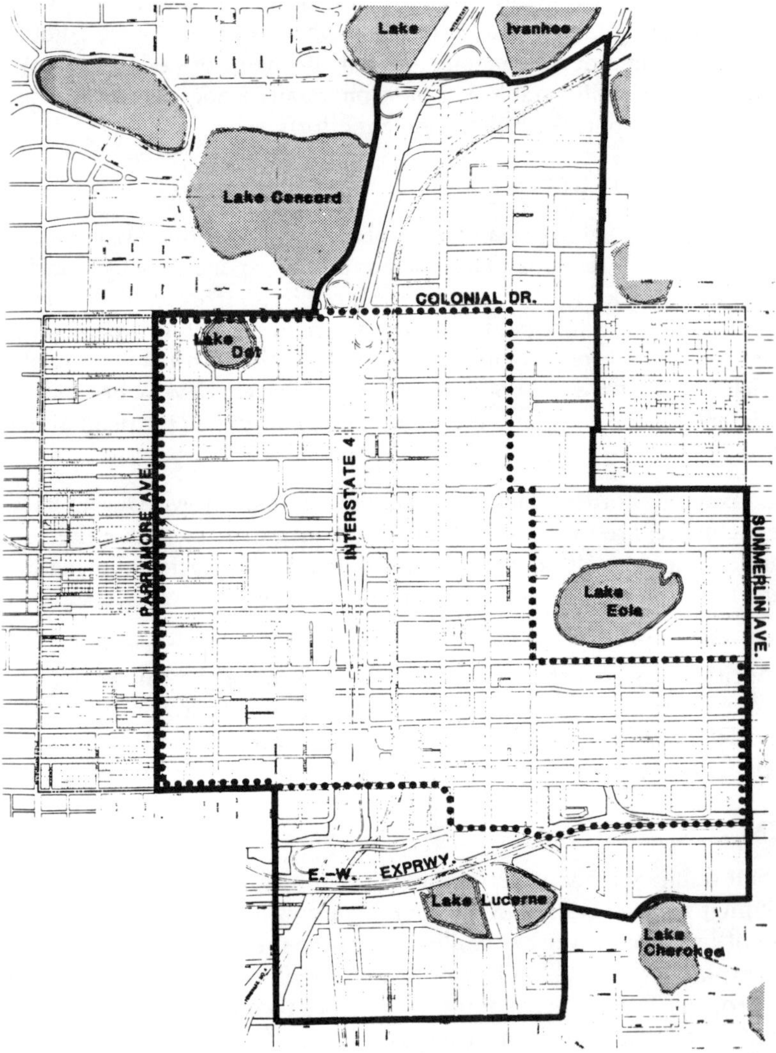

DOWNTOWN DEVELOPMENT DISTRICT

ORLANDO REDEVELOPMENT AREA

5 Ac

0 300 900 2,100 FT.

incremental assessed valuation and taxes was $136.56 million. By the end of the 1984 fiscal year (September 30), the final area valuation was in excess of $237 million; by January, 1985, the assessed value exceeded $363 million. The TIF revenues contributed each year to the trust fund were $940,000 in 1984 and climbed to $2.27 million in FY 1986. Projections for future years indicate annual payments to the trust fund of $2.85 million in FY 1987, growing steadily to $6.00 million in FY 1990. This is based on an increase in property value assessments of $320.36 million by 1990. If projections are restricted to only the most probable of the planned investments, assessed values should increase by $159.8 million, with a concomitant annual payment to the trust fund of approximately $3.0 million by 1990.

Actual achievement of the projected increments in tax revenue depend, of course, on the millage rates adopted by the participating taxing authorities and the realization of anticipated increases in property tax values due to development and redevelopment in the area. The segregation of projects into most probable, probable, and uncertain probability indicates the uncertainty of development plans. Nonetheless, many of the projects are already under way and those in the "probable" category constitute 45 percent of the total; projects labelled "uncertain" account for only 17 percent of the total.

APPLICABILITY

Tax increment financing has been used in other jurisdictions; see, for example, the case studies included above on Davenport, Iowa and Prince George's County, Maryland. TIF district financing is appropriate for areas in which substantial new development is fairly certain to occur in the wake of infrastructure investment. This would imply either new commercial developments or significant upgrading in value and/or density of residential units, thus boosting property values sufficiently to repay the infrastructure costs through tax increments. The TIF districts in Davenport, Iowa and Prince George's County, Maryland supported development of undeveloped land; Orlando's TIF district differs from these since it is composed of land within the urban boundaries and already developed but not developed to its fullest potential.

The disadvantage of tax increment financing in all cases is that, given this dependence on development not yet in place and the fact that millage rates are no different than that for the jurisdiction overall, revenues are not as controllable or certain as, for example, special assessments that are fixed in advance in a special assessment district. Thus care must be taken to accurately project increases in ad valorem tax revenues and match infrastructure expenditures to these revenues or else find supplementary revenue sources.

The advantage of tax increment financing, of course, is the "painlessness" of the exactions -- payment is not added to regular taxes (as with special assessment districts) but rather diverts ad valorem taxes that would have been paid in any case. Further discussion of the advantages and disadvantages of development-based financing and TIF districts in particular are found in Chapter II and the introduction to Chapter III, as well as in discussions of individual case studies in this section.

REFERENCE

Robert R. Garner
Comptroller
City of Orlando
400 South Orange Avenue
Orlando, Florida 32801
Phone (305) 849-2200

DENVER, COLORADO, METROPOLITAN AREA INDEPENDENT TOLL ROAD AUTHORITY

SUMMARY

Toll financing has often been used to finance road construction. This example is unusual since it includes private interests as well as public and because other special revenues are planned to supplement toll revenues in the earlier years.

Recent studies of the transportation network in the greater metropolitan Denver area indicate that current infrastructure is insufficient to support even modest growth in the next 15 years; a 50-mile half-beltway, the E-470, has been proposed as one element to relieve anticipated future congestion. A separate authority, the E-470 Authority, was established to organize planning, construction, operation, and funding of the highway. The effort is a cooperative one involving several counties, a city, and private interests. Financing is anticipated from several sources with tolls constituting a major component.

BACKGROUND

As early as 1958, a beltway around Denver was discussed in the regional plan. Subsequent studies showed the need for the eastern segment. However, it was felt that state and federal funding was not likely to be available for a partial beltway. Nonetheless, local officials and businessmen believed that because many could benefit from such a highway, they could be induced to share in the costs.

Several counties east of Denver had already cooperated in studies of regional transportation needs. In 1983, representatives from Arapahoe, Douglas, and Adams counties, the City of Aurora, and private interests formed the E-470 Task Force. After additional public input was received, the task force published a study in January 1985. Issues reviewed included not only projected traffic demand, but also environmental concerns, physical constraints, current and future land use, and possible financing. The study recommended that the task force become an advisory group to a new intergovernmental agency, the E-470 Authority, which would be responsible for planning, designing, financing, and building the proposed E-470 half-beltway.

The E-470 is planned as a 50-mile long, limited-access highway around the eastern outskirts of Denver, thus diverting through traffic from the urbanized areas and providing access to the planned new Denver International Airport to the northeast. By the year 2015, the E-470 Authority projects that an average of 582,000 weekday trips will use E-470, including 200,000 airport trips.

Construction of the half-beltway is slated to begin during 1988. By 1991, the plan calls for completion of a four-lane controlled-access highway from the southern origination point to the new airport and a two-lane road north to the end of the semicircle. By 1995, plans call for a four-lane road with six lanes in parts.

PROGRAM CHARACTERISTICS

The E-470 Authority is an intergovernmental agency created as a partnership between the public and private sectors. It was created under provisions of the Colorado Public Highway Authority Law which permits such authorities as political subdivisions of the state by contract between any two cities and/or counties within Colorado. The board of directors includes three commissioners from each county and one member of the Aurora city council. The auxiliary executive committee, acting in an advisory capacity, is composed of one member from each of the four public jurisdictions and four developers representing the private sector; two advisors are also appointed.

The estimated cost to complete the highway is $750 million to $950 million. The main criterion in the development of the financial plan is beneficiary financing: money to build the highway should come from those who benefit. Developers with land along the E-470 corridor will profit from increased property values; financing thus includes some recapture of this value as cash and as rights of way contributions. Furthermore, residents and employees of the participating counties and city will benefit through improved access and reduced congestion on existing roads; thus financing includes payment from this group also. Additionally, those who actually travel on the highway, whether residents or passing through, will support the financing through toll charges.

The table below shows the revenue potential of the proposed financial sources and the total debt service for selected years. As debt coverage is required to be a multiple of the debt service, revenue potential far exceeds the actual revenue required. Debt service begins in 1993 and continues for over 30 years at just under $50 million in the earlier years and just over $50 million in the later years.

Financial Projections for Selected Years, $ millions

	1990	1995	2000	2005
Total debt service	0.0	48.6	49.0	49.5
Toll revenues	0.0	22.4	50.9	85.5
County-wide revenues				
Sales tax	15.5	24.1	36.4	53.8
Use tax	1.7	1.9	12.2	14.2
Head tax	20.6	27.5	35.2	43.9
Corridor-wide revenues				
Head tax	0.7	1.6	3.0	4.8
Property tax	6.1	10.0	16.2	24.0
Impact fees	2.6	4.1	4.8	5.0
Corridor-wide, value capture				
Property tax value cap	8.3	21.2	41.4	66.7
Sales tax value cap	0.2	0.3	2.3	3.0
Use tax value cap	0.7	0.8	4.8	5.6

Proposed revenue sources under county jurisdiction include county sales taxes of 0.5 percent and a county use tax of 0.5 percent on 20 percent of sales derived from new construction. Proposed county revenue sources also include a head tax at a level not yet specified; projections presented in the table were based on a head tax of $55 per employee in 1987 with $5 increases every five years.

Revenue sources under the authority's jurisdiction include impact fees of $400 per residential dwelling unit and between $0.25 and $1.00 per nonresidential square foot (depending on building use), an additional head tax within the authority's jurisdictional area of $10 per employee, a 7 mills property tax, and property tax value, sales tax value, and use tax value caps at essentially one-fourth of the county rates.

The most substantial revenue stream in the long run is the projected income from tolls charged to E-470 users. Although limited at the outset, toll revenue is anticipated to exceed debt service by the year 2000. The E-470 Authority hopes to eliminate the county-wide taxes and fees by 1999 and rely on tolls plus corridor-wide taxes and fees until 2007 when it is expected that tolls will be the only revenue source needed.

Moreover, as tolls are expected to grow continuously, it is hoped that the excess over debt service can be used to pay back the local governments, retire the bonds ahead of schedule, and then set up a trust fund of $200 million for perpetual financing of operations and maintenance costs out of interest income. At that time, tolls would be eliminated, the E-470 Authority dissolved, and the E-470 highway given to the state.

EXPERIENCE

This project is still in its formative stages; actual financing and construction have not yet been undertaken.

APPLICABILITY

The laws of other areas may preclude exact replication of the E-470 financing package. However, many of the components of the financing package are already allowed in other jurisdictions. For example, establishment of special financing districts and dedicated jurisdiction-wide special taxes are already permitted in most areas. The uniqueness of the E-470 project is in its public-private partnership and the breadth of financing instruments included in the overall financial plan. The proposed financing combines user-based funding (such as that used in Missoula, Pleasanton, and Fort Collins) with beneficiary-based funding (such as that used in the Denver Mall and Evanston districts) to spread the investment burden among a broad base of the presumed beneficiaries of the road -- both those traveling on the road and those benefitting indirectly through increased property values or economic activity and through reduced congestion on alternate routes. This overall approach to infrastructure financing is transferrable to other areas even if specific components are not.

REFERENCE

John Arnold
Executive Director
The E-470 Authority
7951 East Maplewood Avenue
Suite 324
Englewood, Colorado 80111
Phone (303) 773-9588

IV. EXACTIONS

Exactions may be broadly defined as money, land, or construction services and materials provided by a developer to a public jurisdiction. Traditional exactions include mandatory land dedications for rights of way, parks, and the like, and cash payments in lieu of land. More recently, exactions have been expanded in scope to include donations of specified facilities, construction of off-site infrastructure such as intersections and roads adjacent to the development, addition of low-or moderate-income housing units to the development project, and impact fees and taxes.

Exactions may be offered voluntarily or negotiated individually with each developer when it becomes clear that a project may be delayed or even rejected for want of supporting infrastructure or social amenities. The jurisdiction's power lies in its ability to deny rezoning or refuse building permits for reasons of health, safety, and welfare. Or, a project may be legally permitted but infeasible or undesirable in the absence of public support such as a highway interchange or arterial roadway. In such cases, the developer may volunteer financial or in-kind support to accelerate or substitute for construction by a public authority.

Annexation agreements represent one tool to extract developer concessions. In this case, the local municipality need not rely upon its police or permitting authority in negotiating with an individual developer -- it merely refuses to annex a given area unless certain conditions of infrastructure readiness are met and, if desired, additional contributions to the welfare of the community at large are made. While such fees are justified as compensation for the development's impact on the community, they also may be viewed as a form of "entrance fee."

Exactions may also be assessed on a systematic basis established by local or state legislation with all developers expected to contribute according to a known formula. In addition to on-site infrastructure that may be required as part of the building code, developers may be required to pay impact fees or taxes to compensate the local community for providing off-site services and infrastructure.

In many instances, negotiated exactions precede the use of specified impact fees. There are advantages and disadvantages to each but, when impact fees replace negotiated exactions, it is usually because equality of treatment with impact fees is considered a greater advantage than the flexibility of negotiated exactions that often conflict with (perceived) horizontal equity.

Systematic impact fees, which do not permit developers to negotiate fee levels, can also alter development decisions. Developers unwilling to accept fees at their announced levels may alter their original plans. These types of fees do not permit the local community to change fee structures in response to individual developer circumstances. Chapter II discusses this subject in more detail.

Moreover, in a system that relies on systematic impact fees, variations in infrastructure costs among different developments are not accommodated except as they relate to measured factors such as size and type of development. For example, differences in infrastructure costs due to differences in terrain can only be considered if different impact-fee districts are defined, thus approaching special assessment districts in nature.

Impact fees differ from the fees collected in special assessment districts, described in the previous section, in two major ways. First, impact fee revenues are not as tightly constrained geographically. As with special assessment districts, revenues collected from impact fees may only be used for the types of expenditure targeted. Impact fee revenues, however, may be used anywhere in the collecting jurisdiction whereas assessment district revenues cannot be used outside the defined development area.

Second, systematic impact fees are fixed at the same rate per basic unit (land area, street frontage, housing unit, etc.) for all developers in the jurisdiction. Assessment districts, on the other hand, may contain different fee structures within the same district and may differ from district to district within the same jurisdiction. (Negotiated impact fees, however, do allow for variations among developers and are, in this respect, similar to zoned assessment districts. However, with negotiated impact fees, the variations are not required to be systematic with respect to location or any other objective criterion.)

In general, both impact fees and negotiated exactions offer a beneficiary-based way to finance infrastructure for new development that does not tax existing residents. Because exactions are appropriate only for new development or redevelopment, they are more restricted in applicability than special assessment districts, which can be used in established areas. Like all infrastructure financing dependent upon growth, areas that use exactions must be cautious in their projections so that revenues actually received do not fall short of capital commitments -- a special concern when the fees support bonds.

PREVIEW OF CASES

Of the five cases presented in this section, three focus on impact fees. In Upper Merion Township, Pennsylvania, the fees are used only for road improvements necessitated by new development. In Loveland, Colorado, fees are collected for capital improvements in the more commonly supported areas of water, sewer, stormwater, streets, and electricity, but also for less typical categories such as fire, law enforcement, library and cultural services. The impact fees in Orlando, Florida, are of particular interest not because they cover unusual services but because, even though they are considered a nonrecurring income stream, they have been used to support bond issues.

The fourth case describes a unique variation on negotiated exactions in Napa, California. Developers "bid" for limited building permits by volunteering facility and off-site improvements to enhance their "desirability" ratings. The case is instructive because it describes the characteristics of an unusual approach and also because it notes the reasons this approach was abandoned.

The fifth and last case in this section describes the Corpus Christi, Texas, water and sewer trust funds, which extend the conventional impact fee approach. As in many jurisdictions, water and sewer impact fees paid by developers are based on property frontage with revenues collected deposited in trust funds. Corpus Christi, like other jurisdictions, uses the impact fee system to establish equity of exactions among developers. However, Corpus Christi differs in that it simultaneously transfers the cost-carrying burden from the local jurisdiction to developers. The city requires the first developers in a given area to construct water and sewer facilities sufficient for their project as well as anticipated future development. Reimbursement is from the trust funds but only as funds become available -- thus developers may not receive full repayment until subsequent developers have paid enough into the trust funds to cover investment costs.

UPPER MERION TOWNSHIP, PENNSYLVANIA TRANSPORTATION DEVELOPMENT DISTRICT

SUMMARY

Upper Merion Township, a suburb of Philadelphia, created a transportation development district (TDD) to ensure that new development helps pay for road improvements. The TDD allows the township to charge impact fees based on the number of trips generated by new development, with the revenues dedicated to transportation improvements.

BACKGROUND

Upper Merion Township (which includes King of Prussia) is a fast-growing suburb about 15 miles west of Philadelphia. Major roads, including the Pennsylvania Turnpike, Schuylkill Expressway, and Route 202 have made this area a desirable location for residential, industrial, and commercial development. The resulting growth in population and development mean that the road system has problems in accommodating the volume of traffic. Between 1975 and 1985, the population grew by 8.47 percent to 28,263.

While the township has a good credit rating, it wanted to keep its bonding ability for other capital needs. Further, Pennsylvania's Department of Transportation was not in a financial position to provide the more than $30 million required for these road improvements. As a result, Upper Merion officials examined ways to raise revenue on their own.

The solution proposed by township officials was the Upper Merion Highway/Traffic Improvement Program. The ordinance, approved by the Board of Supervisors, was developed by a traffic task force composed of representatives from the township, industry, the Chamber of Commerce, regional planning boards, representatives from the Pennsylvania Department of Transportation as well as a citizen's advisory board. Public hearings were held by the task force. The idea for this program originated within the township, but its legal foundation was strengthened under the Pennsylvania Transportation Partnership Act (August 1985).

PROGRAM CHARACTERISTICS

The Highway/Traffic Capital Improvement Program has four basic components:

- A transportation development district--in this case, it encompasses the entire Upper Merion Township area.
- An inventory of road improvements needed to meet current and future traffic demand. This listing includes estimates of construction costs, expected improvements to traffic flows, and related issues.
- A fee based on total improvement costs, land use, and traffic expected to be generated from each development. This process allocates the improvement

costs according to the amount of traffic expected to be generated by each new development.

- A highway/traffic capital improvement fund under the control of the township. Fees received from developers are deposited into the fund with disbursements made on a pay-as-you-go basis. Disbursements can provide the full cost of the highway improvements or provide the local match for federal, state, or other grants.

The most important aspect of the improvement program is the fee imposed on developers. The first step in fee assessment is the calculation of "unit improvement cost." This is simply the total cost estimate to construct highway improvements under the program divided by the increase in peak-hour traffic capability provided by the new construction.

Traffic studies showed that completing all needed highway construction and road improvements for the township would cost $33.3 million but would increase the capacity to handle peak-hour traffic by some 17,930 vehicles.

Combining these figures shows a capital cost of $1,860 per increased peak-hour vehicle. This number was reduced by 50 percent to account for expected federal, state, county, and local funding programs as well as the additional traffic generated by interstate and regional highway improvements. The resulting unit improvement cost for private developers is thus $930 per vehicle. In other words, a developer is assessed $930 for each vehicle his particular project is expected to generate. This assessment is adjusted annually to reflect the impact of inflation on construction costs.

The second step in fee assessment is the calculation of each new development's expected contribution to traffic. Estimates of peak hour vehicles generated by various developments are based on research conducted by the Institute of Transportation Engineers (ITE). A single-family, detached home is projected to generate one trip during peak hours and therefore would pay $930 per unit. A retirement community is expected to average only 0.40 vehicles per dwelling unit and thus would pay $386 per unit. A hospital is expected to generate 1.27 trips per patient and would pay $1,225 per bed, while a nursing home is only expected to generate 0.21 trips and would pay $203 per bed.

Fees are also specified for other land use categories including hotels ($820 per room or $849 per employee), racquet clubs ($3,956 per court), general office space ($2.72 per square foot), and industrial parks ($0.96 per square foot or $550 per employee).

EXPERIENCE

Although the program has only been in operation for a year and a half, more than $3 million has already been raised. Two road projects are under way, and a third is being planned using the revenue raised under the program to meet the local match required for federal highway grants.

To date, no major problems have been encountered with the program, although a group of developers did try to convince the state legislature to change the underlying legislation. Some bureaucratic difficulties have arisen due to federal involvement, more specifically, concerning use of the revenue as the local match for federal funds. Most problems, however, were worked out during an extensive planning process. For example, a traffic coordination committee was established to address highway changes that affected neighboring townships.

APPLICABILITY

Theoretically, this type of program could be implemented in a wide variety of places. Other townships in Pennsylvania are currently developing similar transportation development districts. Two drawbacks, however, could make this exact program unsuitable in some situations.

First, not all local governments possess the legal, administrative, and institutional arrangements to implement such a program. Townships in Pennsylvania are relatively autonomous, with a large degree of independent taxing power and authority. Local governments in other states may not possess such authority and have to obtain state approval by means of legislation or referendum. Some local government entities with adequate authority may still need to secure popular approval in a town meeting or another local referendum.

Second, transportation development districts have the same disadvantage as all approaches that rely on special fees collected from new entrants: they may work only in fast growing areas. Areas not experiencing rapid growth might not be able to charge such "entrance" fees because developers could locate in communities that do not impose them. For more discussion of this, see the section on market sensitivity in Chapter II.

This program, besides allowing local governments to raise revenue from those who are contributing to the problem, also reduces the dependence of local governments on federal and state revenue sources. This gives area officials more control over their road and highway systems.

REFERENCES

Ronald Wagenmann
Upper Merion Township Manager
Phone (215) 265-8722

Benjamin Myers
Assistant to the Township Manager
Phone (215) 265-2600
Upper Merion Township
175 West Valley Forge Road
King of Prussia, Pennsylvania 19406

LOVELAND, COLORADO IMPACT FEES

SUMMARY

Loveland, Colorado, charges development fees to ensure that new users pay for the services they require. These impact fees are structured to reflect the actual costs of expanding services and are intended to be neutral with respect to the pace and type of development. This approach is of particular interest because the program was designed to also include services not usually covered by impact fees, such as general government, police, fire, and recreational services.

BACKGROUND

Loveland is a city of approximately 37,000 persons on 19.6 square miles of land in the Fort Collins Metropolitan Statistical Area (MSA). Between 1970 and 1980, Loveland grew at an annual rate of 8.8 percent; total city area doubled during the period. The broader Fort Collins MSA was itself the fourth fastest-growing MSA in the country in that decade. Since 1980, however, Loveland's population growth has slowed to 3 percent annually, though total city area has continued to grow through annexation at a faster rate.

Loveland's primary industrial base is high-technology; the largest employer is Hewlett-Packard with approximately 2,500 employees. The reduced rate of population growth in Loveland is part of the economic slowdown along Colorado's Front Range. The collapse of the oil and gas industry (including the demise of the oil shale industry on the Western Slope) and the recession in high technology industries are the leading forces behind this economic shift.

In recent years, revenues accruing to the city government have not grown as rapidly as the demand for services and expenditures, particularly for capital expansion. Given Loveland's expectations for future growth, there was concern that the general fund would be unable to adequately finance the required expansion in services. Furthermore, there was a general feeling that the costs to expand service capacity should be borne by the new users in proportion to benefits received. In response, the city council started the Service Cost Recovery System project in June 1982. Consultants were retained and a citizen's Cost of Growth Advisory Committee was established to assist in setting up a system in which new development would "buy in" to the existing service system by paying impact-type fees.

The city council adopted several general guidelines for the Service Cost Recovery System:

- New development should pay the costs of general fund services provided as well as for utility services;
- Service levels for new development should be the same as those provided to existing users;

- Funds collected from new development should benefit new development; and
- Timing of fees should be related to timing of demand for services.

These principles should ensure that capital costs are correctly attributed to the growth that requires the increased capacity, acknowledging that different types of development impose different levels of demand for services. Furthermore, the system is structured so that new and existing residents pay the same amount for the same service levels: that is, there should be no cross-subsidies between new and existing residents. However, variations according to geographical location and type of development were not implemented because it was felt that the additional complexity and costs involved did not justify any improved efficiency.

PROGRAM CHARACTERISTICS

Loveland's development fees have two parts: one-time fees associated with utility hook-ups (water, sewer, etc.) and capital expansion fees (CEFs) that support services handled through the general fund. Charges to support utility service capacity expansion are treated separately in the Loveland Municipal Code where, in addition to hook-up fees, payment of facilities expansion fees are detailed.

The CEFs introduced with the Service Cost Recovery System include only the growth-related component of such services as parks and recreation, fire protection, law enforcement, streets, and general government and cultural services. CEFs reflect demand for expanded net capacity and do not include costs to replace or upgrade existing facilities. These latter are included in the operating budget funded by both old and new residents equally.

Because services financed through the general fund are not metered or otherwise monitored for benefits actually received, CEFs are calculated using surrogates to determine relative benefits. The base unit and charge per unit are the same for each user within a given user category. The capital costs required for expansion are derived from an annual capital improvement program (adjusted to net out replacement and betterment costs). These costs are then allocated to the residential, commercial, and industrial sectors according to expected benefits. Each sector's capital cost burden is divided by the anticipated increase in the relevant unit factor--number of housing units for residential, square footage for commercial, acreage for industrial--to arrive at the CEF per unit appropriate to each sector.

Fees are based upon current replacement costs and reflect the marginal cost to replicate a unit of infrastructure necessary to service an additional user (sometimes called "vintage" pricing). New residents moving in after a given capital expansion but before a planned expansion pay a CEF based on current facility costs -- that is, more than the actual costs incurred for the past expansion but less than that expected for the future additional expansion. Fees are updated annually to reflect changes in costs.

The CEFs paid by new residents go either toward retiring debt on previously developed facilities or into an escrow account for future facility construction. Each CEF component is earmarked for a specific infrastructure expenditure -- streets, libraries, etc. -- and must be spent within that category. In recognition of the uneven timing of such expenditures, however, borrowing among funds is permitted.

Current CEFs (which exclude utility expansion and hook-up fees) are $1,537 per residential unit, $0.93 per square foot for commercial developments, and $4,550 per acre for industrial developments (see table).

Capital Expansion Fees by Service

	Residential (per unit)	Commercial (per sq.ft.)	Industrial (per acre)
Parks and recreation	$ 736	--	--
Fire	98	$ 0.07	$ 746
Police	24	0.02	179
Library and museum	179	--	--
General government	271	0.19	2,024
Streets	229	0.65	1,601
Total	$1,537	$ 0.93	$4,550

In addition to the CEFs, new developments are charged utility fees that include a capital or plant investment component. Sewer plant investment fees vary with tap diameter; water plant investment fees vary with tap diameter and, for residential units, lot area net of improvements. Electric plant investment fees vary according to the type of user; there is a one-time flat fee per residential unit. Non-residential users pay an incremental fee per kilowatt hour which is deposited in an electric utilities expansion fund.

Utility plant development and hook-up fees plus permit fees constitute more than 75 percent while CEFs account for less than 25 percent of the $6,642 in total development fees for a typical single-family residential unit; for a typical commercial property CEFs constitute 43 percent of total development charges of $62,021 (see table). The table excludes electric facility expansion fees since non-residential users pay these over extended periods. The calculations are based on a 2,000 square-foot, single-family, residential

Examples of Total Development Fees

	Single Family	Office/Industrial
Water/sewer	$4,593	$28,424
Permit fees	374	3,939
Storm drainage	138	2,968
All CEFs	1,537	26,690
Total development fees	$6,642	$62,021

unit, quarter acre lot, and a 4-acre office/industrial development--15,000 square feet office space, 2.8 acres light industrial space.

EXPERIENCE

By the end of 1986, approximately $2.2 million had been collected in CEFs since collections commenced in July 1984. Annual revenue from CEFs equals about 10 percent of the income to the general fund.

With several years experience, two shortcomings of the CEF structure have been observed: (1) funding for storm drainage is insufficient, and (2) timing of CEF receipts does not always correlate well with timing of needed infrastructure investments. This latter is a special problem for streets, since construction is usually undertaken before development occurs and therefore before payment of the CEF. Solutions to both problems are currently being investigated.

Initially, CEFs were collected when builders received certificates of occupancy or 120 days after building permits were issued. However, this schedule created collection problems. Builders expect to be charged fees at permitting time and set aside funds accordingly; but with CEF collection deferred, builders were often caught in a cash squeeze either because the finished project had not yet been sold or because they had not set aside sufficient funds in anticipation of CEF assessment. In fact, the CEF delinquency rate reached as high as 20 percent and the city became a collection agency. Furthermore, since not all lenders require certificates of occupancy, some builders were overlooked and thus not assessed CEFs.

Because of these problems, the collection system was revised in January 1987, and Loveland now collects the CEFs when building permits are issued. In addition to full coverage of builders and higher collection rates under the new system, fees are received earlier in the development process, thus improving Loveland's cash position.

Loveland monitors the potential impact of CEFs on development by regularly comparing total development fees imposed by Loveland with those imposed by nearby jurisdictions not imposing the full range of capital development fees (i.e., excluding general government, fire, police, and cultural activities). In a 1987 comparison, Loveland's total fees were significantly below those of Longmont (largely due to high water and sewer fees), above those of Greeley, and less than 5 percent above those of Fort Collins.

Nonetheless, the city decided to rebate CEFs for new industry as a result of a burden/benefit analysis of new industry. This study concluded that the fiscal benefits from industry payment of property taxes, use of city utilities, etc., were greater than the incremental CEF-associated burden. However, though the CEFs were essentially eliminated in an effort to attract new industry, the city was careful to maintain the integrity of the CEF revenues available for infrastructure by itself paying into the funds the shortfall created by the new industry rebate. Specifically, the city calculates the net fiscal benefit of each new industry locating in Loveland (new revenues created less infrastructure costs) and pays that amount into the CEF funds on behalf of the industry, thus maintaining the financial health of the funds.

APPLICABILITY

Loveland's extension of impact fee financing to underwrite the costs of public services as well as conventional physical infrastructure is innovative. Its use in other jurisdictions may be constrained by local laws that do not permit distinctions between established residents and new landowners. However, the real constraint on impact fees for community services is probably the developers themselves and their reaction to the total level of fees, however earmarked. Loveland explicitly recognizes the possible market effects of impact fees and, as a result, periodically assesses its position vis-a-vis its geographical competitors. (For a more detailed discussion of effect of fees on developer response, see the section on market sensitivity in Chapter II.)

REFERENCES

Greg Demko
Director
Department of Administrative Services

James H. Hannah
Director
Department of Planning, Engineering, and Building
City of Loveland
410 East Fifth Street
Loveland, Colorado 80537
Phone (303) 667-6130

ORLANDO, FLORIDA
BONDED IMPACT FEES

SUMMARY

Beginning in 1984, Orlando issued several revenue bonds to finance expansion and improvement of its wastewater treatment system. These bonds were secured in part by wastewater system impact fees. Although many cities in Florida and other states have impact fees, the use of impact fees as bond security makes Orlando's program unique.

BACKGROUND

The City of Orlando is part of the three-county Orlando Metropolitan Statistical Area (MSA) consisting of Orange, Osceola, and Seminole Counties. The city itself accounted for 143,000, or 17 percent, of the MSA population in 1985. Prior to 1967, the economy was based upon agriculture and citrus products, tourism, light manufacturing, and space-related industries tied to the Kennedy Space Center. The area also serves as a major distribution center for the Florida peninsula.

In the last ten years, Orlando has become home not only to Disney World and other tourist attractions but also to increasing convention activity. Thus, compared to the nation as a whole, Orlando has a larger than average share of employment in the trade and service sectors. Orlando has also experienced a higher than average growth in high technology industries, up 114 percent since 1976 compared to a 40 percent increase nationally. In addition, several well-known manufacturing companies have their headquarters in the Orlando area.

Between 1970 and 1985, the MSA population increased by 90 percent to nearly 862,000; a significant portion of this increment was in the prime working age group of 25-44 year olds. By 1990 this age group is projected to expand by another 47.5 percent and total MSA population should exceed one million.

Given this expected rapid growth, it was clear that utilities such as wastewater treatment would have to be expanded significantly. Maximum capacity of the two major and one lesser treatment plants in the system serving Orlando and several surrounding communities was somewhat less than 44 million gallons per day (MGD) in 1985. Billable flows are projected to reach this by level 1988 and to exceed 50 MGD by 1991.

The Orlando wastewater system has already begun improvements at the two larger plants to increase capacity and to comply with discharge standards. In addition, new lines to improve collection and to better integrate the two major treatment plants will be installed. These investments are being funded in part by federal grants, with the balance financed by the system itself and by the several governmental jurisdictions in proportion to their share in the incremental capacity.

Orlando's share of the planned improvements totals close to $230 million. Of this, nearly $53 million will be met through federal grants and $12.6 million from the system itself, leaving somewhat more than $164 million to be funded with bond proceeds and investment earnings.

PROGRAM CHARACTERISTICS

In July 1983, Orlando authorized a borrowing program to finance the costs of the overall improvement in the wastewater system. Several bond issues were floated beginning in 1984. Although impact fees were collected in Orlando previously, they were first pledged as security for a bond issue in 1984. As of April 1986, wastewater impact fees were $6.25 per gallon per day of capacity. Total initial wastewater fees in 1986 for in-city single-family residences were $2,267 composed of $1,969 in impact fees (including pollution control charges) and a $298 connection fee (including lateral collection system connection fee, inspection fees, and front footage fees).

The channeling of impact fees to debt service is neither simple nor direct. The flow of general revenues, impact fees, and utilities taxes through their respective accounts to the various user accounts is diagrammed in the flow of funds chart presented below.

Specifically, gross revenues of the system itself (monthly user charges, for example) are deposited into the General Revenue Account and one-time impact fees are deposited into the Impact Fee Account. In turn, revenues from the General Revenue Account, are transferred to the Operations and Maintenance Account to pay for the system's functioning. As specified in the bond prospectus, a portion is then available for transfer into the Debt Service Account to support interest payments and, then, into various reserve and refunding reserve accounts.

Impact fees flow through the Impact Fee Account to the expansion project component of the Senior Bond Debt Service Account. However, impact fees deposited to this account cannot exceed the proportion of total senior debt service attributable to expansion projects. Currently, 72 percent of senior bonds outstanding are for expansion projects and 28 percent for improvement projects. Impact fees over and above this limit are allocated to the Senior Bond Reserve Account if a deficit exists in this account -- the residual impact fee revenues are then transferred to the Impact Fee Stabilization Account. The overflow from this latter account may be used directly by the city to support wastewater system investments after other requirements are satisfied.

Revenues from the Utilities Service Tax (levied on the purchase of electricity, fuel oil, metered and bottled gas, water and telecommunication services) are paid by the city into the Utilities Tax Account for a specified holding period and thus serve as additional security for debt servicing. If not required for debt servicing, these funds are deposited into the general fund.

In addition to these revenues, investment funds are also collected via the monthly water bills as fixed capital fees per household ($8) or commercial unit ($34.75) for in-city units and 50 percent higher for out-of-city units. Capital fees collected from "old customers" (those already in the system by the end of 1983) are earmarked for system improvements. Capital fees from "new customers" (those entering the system after 1983) are added to the Impact Fee Account for investments to expand the system.

ORLANDO

Flow of Funds

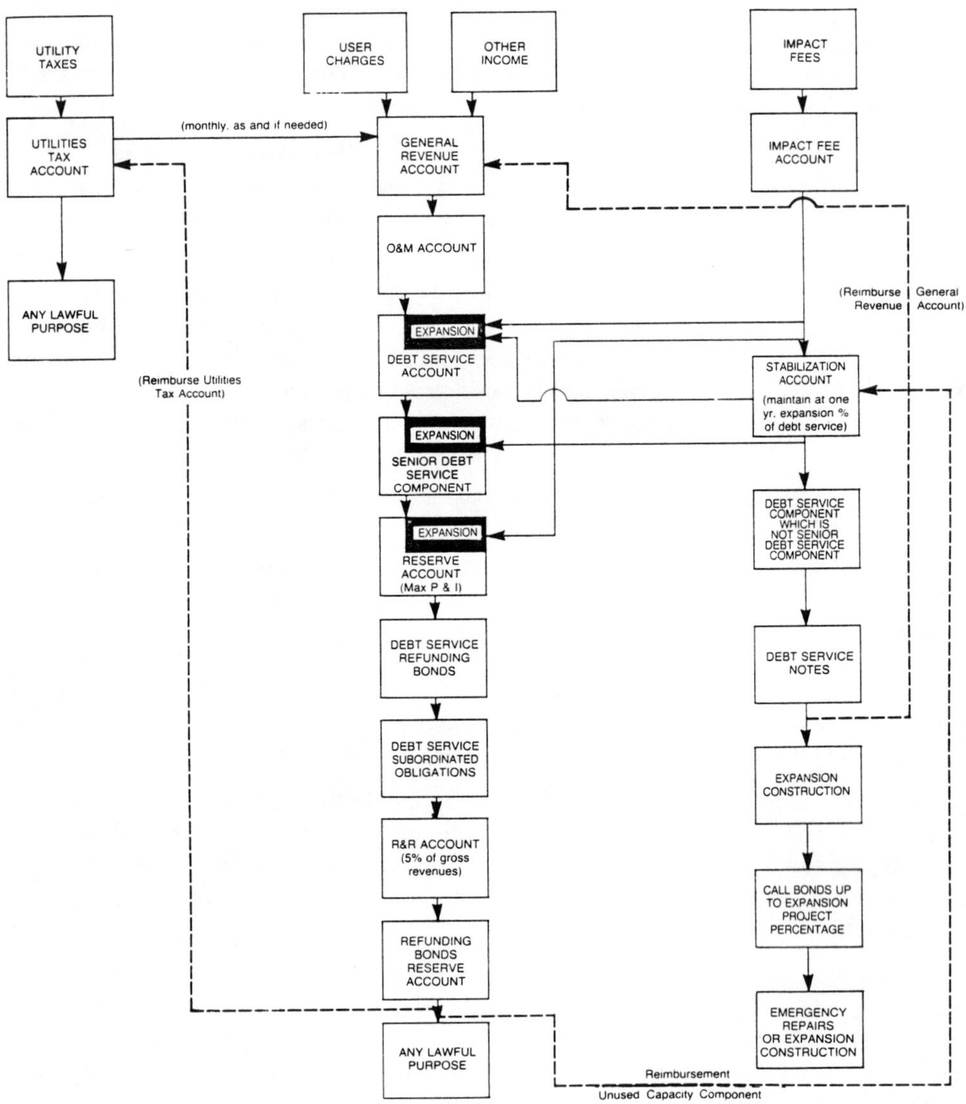

EXPERIENCE

New revenue from impact fees was anticipated to be $7.5 million in the fiscal year ended September 30, 1986. However, the amount transferred to the Debt Account in any one year may exceed impact fee revenues collected in that year. Thus, impact fee funds available for debt service were expected to be $11.4 million since impact fee revenues accumulate in the Impact Fee Account. Overall, it was expected that close to $35 million would be available to pay $21.4 million in debt service in the 1986 fiscal year, with the remainder accounted for by $12.6 million in net revenues of the system and $10.9 million from utilities services taxes.

Orlando's total wastewater connection fees (including impact fees) are high for single-family residences and were exceeded in 1986 by only two of the 12 jurisdictions in the area competing with Orlando for new development. This, however, is mitigated by the low monthly rates charged by Orlando relative to these same jurisdictions. In any case, the level of impact fees has not appeared to deter development in Orlando as shown by a substantial waiting list for sewer connections.

APPLICABILITY

The use of impact fees is not unique to Orlando; there are many jurisdictions in Florida alone charging impact fees. However, Orlando is unusual in its use of impact fees as partial security for revenue bonds. Its system of carefully segregated accounts and tied revenues ensures that impact fees and capacity fees are used only for investments related to the needs of those who pay these fees. Moreover, the bonds are backed with an insurance policy guaranteeing payments; insurance costs on the impact-fee supported issues were 1.40-1.77 percent of principal and the insured bonds were assigned a AAA rating.

Nonetheless, not all jurisdictions are able to support bond issues with non-recurring revenues, such as impact fees. In jurisdictions that limit bond security to recurring revenues, only fees such as Orlando's monthly capacity fees would be allowed as bond security. It is possible, however, that bond insurance and special enabling legislation would allow other jurisdictions to implement financing similar to Orlando's.

The advantages and disadvantages of Orlando's program parallel those associated with all financing approaches dependent upon growth to generate investment funds: market sensitivity to fees and the possibility of growth and revenues falling short of expectations.

REFERENCE

Robert R. Garner
Comptroller
400 South Orange Avenue
Orlando, Florida 32801
Phone (305) 849-22007

NAPA, CALIFORNIA
COMPETITIVE EXACTIONS

SUMMARY

In Napa, California, the city council adopted a residential development management program to restrict the rate of growth. Anticipating a demand for building permits greater than that allowed under the program, the city council established a system to evaluate building plans and to award building permits to those deemed most desirable. In order to improve their evaluation score, many builders offered ("bid") to supply elements of infrastructure at their own expense.

BACKGROUND

In 1975, the Napa city council adopted a general plan that called for a population of 75,000 by the year 2000. A study prepared three years later by the Department of Planning and Community Development projected that target might be reached 10-14 years earlier. This expectation was based on the existing rate of growth in Napa.

The city council supported its call for restrictions on growth with the results of a June 1978 referendum in which 69 percent of the Napa city residents voted to limit population in the county to under 115,000 by the year 2000. The council felt that support of this referendum for a county population limit could be interpreted as a population limit of 75,000 for the city within the Residential Urban Limit Line.

In order to control growth and to ensure the quality of the growth that was allowed, the city council created a residential development management program in which a predetermined number of building permits were issued each year to applicants rating the highest on a scale of development qualities.

PROGRAM CHARACTERISTICS

The number of building permits to be issued each year was calculated as a function of the annual increment in population to reach the target, the average population per household, and the vacancy factor. In turn, this limited number of building permits was awarded to the applicants with the highest score in the competitive evaluation process.

Applicants were evaluated on a number of factors, some of which could be effectively altered by the applicant himself such as the existence of a sidewalk running from the proposed development to the nearest elementary school. The city council published a list of points to be awarded for each criterion or quality factor. For example, projects with a continuous improved walkway to the assigned public elementary school were awarded 2 points; developments lacking a walkway or having only an incomplete sidewalk were granted no points. Other criteria included proximity to fire stations, central business district, city bus route, and public parks; existence of continuous walkways by most direct route to the closest retail shopping facility and parks; quality of traffic flow and circulation; housing types, design, and mixture; and provision of open space and common recreational facilities.

Builders could effectively improve their competitive rating by offering to provide, at their own expense, additions that were deemed desirable such as off-site sidewalks, recreational facilities, road access, and the like. In one application, for example, the developer agreed to acquire and dedicate a public easement and construct a pathway to a nearby park at his own expense and, also, to construct a cul-de-sac off-site between his project and a city street. At one point, there were apparently on-the-spot additions made by developers to their applications as they were reviewed in open council hearings. The system was in essence a **competitive auction** for limited permits in which developers offered exactions to boost their ratings.

EXPERIENCE

The Napa system was abandoned in 1980 after one year of operation. The experience did prove that developers were willing to invest more than they had previously in infrastructure and in increasing the desirable qualities of their projects. However, the excessive pressure for growth did not materialize, and there was no need to continue to limit building permits to such a degree.

Moreover, the system proved to be administratively unwieldy and difficult to manage. As a result, the staff was not unhappy when it was abandoned. There was neither sufficient time nor staff to critically evaluate the feasibility of the offers of greater amenities. For example, a developer-proposed sidewalk involved crossing farmland not owned by the developer or the city; after the city had accepted the application, the farmer refused permission for the sidewalk to be built across his farm. Off-site road widening investments offered by developers also were refused because the city did not own the rights of way and the landowners along the proposed route did not want a wider road passing their homes leading to a new development.

APPLICABILITY

The competition for building permits in force in Napa could be used in other jurisdictions in which demand for permits exceeds the supply considered desirable given local development plans. However, it will work only when demand is strong and the exactions asked from developers are not so great that growth is discouraged and diverted to other localities. In this sense, the reservations associated with this type of program are much the same as those associated with any program involving exactions (either in-kind or cash) from developers. Certainly, the offers made by developers should be reviewed more critically than was the case in Napa, to ensure that they are in fact feasible and desirable before points and building permits are awarded.

Napa's approach is a variation of negotiated exactions, contrasting with the systematic impact fees used in Upper Merion Township, Loveland, and Orlando (detailed above). Like other negotiated exactions, its flexibility in dealing with developers allowed consideration of market sensitivity in setting exaction levels. The Napa approach, however, differs from other forms of negotiated exactions because there was no individual bargaining or differentiation in standards among developers. All "negotiations" for permits to be issued within a given time period were conducted simultaneously and the criteria for evaluation were stated in advance. Any increases in exactions were offered openly, in front of other developers. Because there were no exceptions made to stated criteria and developers were free to change development specifications to garner increased points, the inequities associated with other negotiated exactions could be avoided (in theory).

REFERENCE

John W. Lindblad
Public Works Director
City of Napa
P.O. Box 660
Napa, California 94559
Phone (707) 252-7711

CORPUS CHRISTI, TEXAS WATER AND SEWER TRUST FUNDS

SUMMARY

Corpus Christi is of interest because it is not a fast-growing city and has tried a series of tactics to finance its public works, including several city-wide, modal trust funds--an unusual and more flexible variation on impact fees.

Prior to 1982, Corpus Christi financed new water and sewer lines on an ad hoc basis; sometimes the city installed new lines, sometimes developers installed them at their own expense. There was no systematic method to ensure that each developer was responsible for his fair share of the costs. To better manage investment in water and sewer systems, the city created four trust funds, two each in water and sewer. The trusts receive specified portions of the fees paid by developers; in turn, these funds are used to reimburse developers and the city for construction of necessary water and sewer lines.

BACKGROUND

Located on the Texas Gulf Coast, Corpus Christi had a 1986 population of close to 267,000. Total area of the city is 396 square miles; of this, 277 square miles are water that produce considerable revenues from oil and gas properties. Its port has been approved as a site for the first federal trade zone in the United States to permit petroleum refiners to operate using full zone privileges; users of the zone will be permitted to defer custom duties on imports and, in some cases, avoid duties, tariffs, and excise taxes on certain exports. The city hopes that this will benefit the local economy, which has been hurt by the recent decline in the price of oil.

The city created various enterprise funds to account for activities that render services on a fee basis. These funds are expected to be financially self-sufficient and include water, gas, wastewater and transit systems, the airport, emergency medical services, and a golf center. Within the water and wastewater enterprise funds, the city set up special trust accounts to ensure proper funding and construction of the water and sewer lines necessary to serve new developments within the city.

Prior to establishment of the water and sewer trusts, there was no set policy as to who underwrote the cost to construct lines to service new developments. Sometimes the city put in the lines at its own cost; sometimes developers built the lines at their own cost. Regardless of how they were financed initially, subsequent developments could tie into these lines without reimbursing the builders. Although the city usually installed and paid for the largest mains, the lack of a consistent policy led to inequities in financing with later developments paying less than their fair share.

As a result of disaffection with this ad hoc system, the city began reimbursing developers when they "oversized" mains or increased sewer depth to accommodate anticipated future developments (Fort Collins, Colorado, has a similar policy of reimbursing developers for oversizing). Nonetheless, this system was not considered truly satisfactory and, in 1981, the city created a commission to work out a more equitable policy.

The commission -- composed of city staff, consulting engineers, land developers and home builders, and a few private citizens -- proposed the ordinances that now effectively govern the water and sewer trust funds. The Water Ordinance was approved and became effective in June 1982, and the Sanitary Sewer Ordinance in December 1982. There was insufficient consensus among commission members, particularly developers, to agree on a structure for a storm drainage trust.

PROGRAM CHARACTERISTICS

Four trust funds were established by the 1982 ordinances, one each for major and supporting water lines and for major and supporting sewer lines. These trusts provide a closer link between those who benefit from the new lines and those who pay for them. All developers pay into the trusts whether they are the first or the last to develop property in an area; all developers who construct water and/or sewer lines which will be used by subsequent developments are reimbursed from the trust funds for the costs they incur.

The city's Platting Ordinance defines the fees to be paid into the four trusts; current fee levels were specified in the 1984 ordinance. There are three types of fees: lot/acreage, surcharge, and pro rata. First, each developer is assessed a **fixed fee** per lot or per acre, whichever is greater, for each of the two functional areas (water and sewer). Second, developers are also assessed an additional sanitary sewer **surcharge** per lot for all types of construction and a water **surcharge** for single-family or duplex residential construction. Last, developers tapping into distribution and/or collection lines that have been constructed by other developers or the city must pay into the appropriate trust funds a **pro rata** charge per foot of line fronting their property.

To account for inflation, fee levels are indexed to the August Construction Index published in **Engineering News Record.** Lot/acreage and pro rata fees are paid prior to the signing of the final plat; unit surcharges are paid at the time tap fees are paid. In 1984, the combined lot/acreage and surcharge fees amounted to $425/lot or $900/acre plus $200/lot for single-family and duplex construction. For all other construction, the 1984 combined lot/acreage and surcharge fees were $400/lot or $1,200/acre plus $100/lot. The allocation of these fees to the two trust funds in each area (water and sewer) is presented schematically in the figure below.

The funds from these four trusts are then available to pay the city for water and sewer line construction and to reimburse developers for construction beyond the public works for which they are directly responsible. The Platting Ordinance limits reimbursements to developers to construction within city plans and standards; reimbursements (fee credits plus cash) are specified in the ordinance and are, in essence, proportional to the fees paid by the developer. For example, if a property is developed near an existing water grid but not immediately adjacent to the grid main, the maximum off-site water line extension that will be funded by the trust is one half mile. In payment for off-site construction, developers can be credited with their full fee liability and, in addition, reimbursed

FLOW OF FUNDS: WATER AND SEWER TRUST FUND

CORPUS CHRISTI, TEXAS

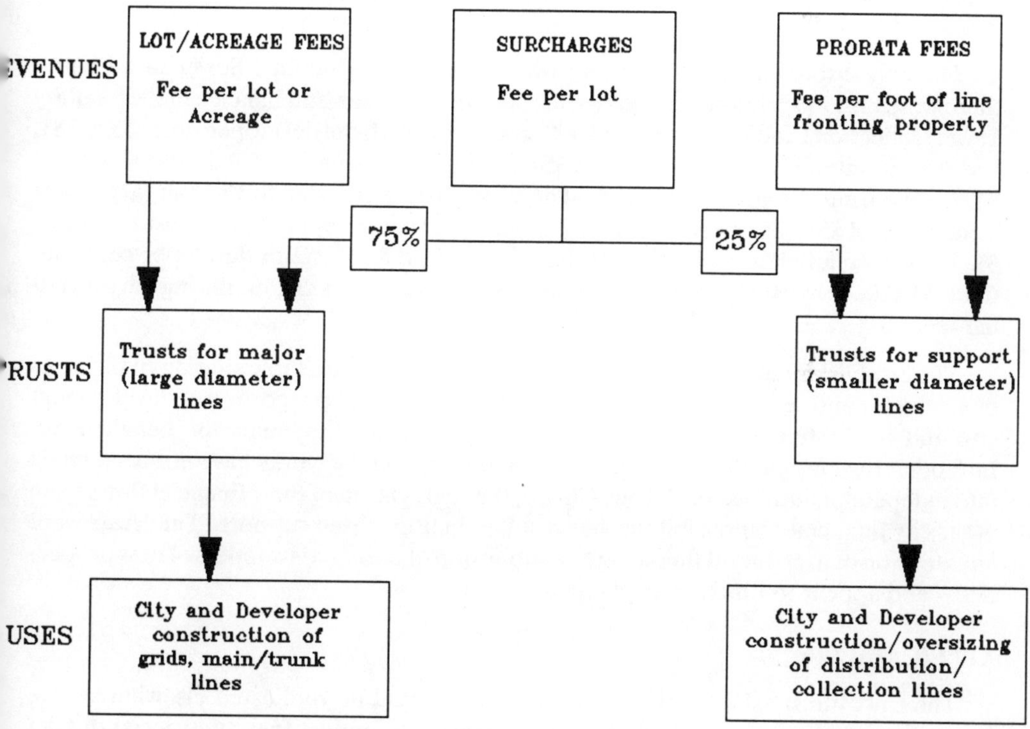

in cash from the trusts up to an amount equal to half the total costs; any costs beyond this total (that is, half of total costs plus full fee value) must be borne by the developer.

Similarly, limits on credit and reimbursement are specified for construction of off-site sewer collection lines. Although developers are reimbursed in full for construction of trunk lines, reimbursements for collection line extensions are limited to the following maximum:

Maximum = 0.5(average pipe diameter)(fee value)

Developers are also compensated for the incremental costs of oversizing beyond an eight-inch diameter line.

EXPERIENCE

As of July 31, 1986, there was a balance of $104,166 in the Sanitary Sewer (Main) Trust Fund; receipts for the fiscal year were $6,600 in developer contributions and $5,658 in interest.

The only disbursement for the year was $30,757 to the Sanitary Sewer Bond Fund; there were no 1986 reimbursements to developers. The year-end balance in the Sanitary Sewer Collection Line Trust was $274,488; contributions from developers were $379,381, investment interest income was $12,854, and reimbursements to developers were $277,599 during the preceding year. There was also a transfer to the Sanitary Sewer Bond Fund of $57,370 during the same period. The Water Supply Main Trust had a July 31, 1986 closing balance of $274,488, having received $221,052 in developer contributions, $34,106 in interest income, and reimbursed developers $233,588 during the preceding year.

The establishment of the four trusts has meant a more equitable sharing of the costs of new water and sewer lines. All developers are assessed in proportion to development size and are systematically reimbursed for expenditures they make on behalf of future/other developments. Although water and sewer public works have not been made into independent utilities in Corpus Christi, the segregation of their financial flows from other city financial responsibilities has resulted in user-based support. The trusts were an extension of user-based financing to a sub-group of users -- developers of new properties -- and appear to function as planned.

APPLICABILITY

The trust funds established in Corpus Christi could be replicated elsewhere. The fees collected, though not titled as such, are similar to impact fees and special district assessments and are used in much the same way -- to build infrastructure in support of new development. Corpus Christi, however, is not geographically restricted in the use of the trust fund revenues. Thus, the city has more flexibility in allocation of funds than would be allowed in assessment or special improvement districts created for similar financing where all funds collected must be reinvested in the same geographically defined district. The flexibility of trust funds similar to those in Corpus Christi, based on impact-type fees, might therefore be administratively advantageous to a city in which development is occurring in several non-adjacent areas simultaneously and in which there are no independent water and sewer utilities.

REFERENCES

Victor Medina
Director of Engineering Services

Debra Andrews
Director of Finance
City of Corpus Christi
P.O. Box 9277
Corpus Christi, Texas 78469-9277
Phone (512) 880-3000

V. UTILITIES

A number of governments have segregated public works activities into independent utilities that oversee all aspects of the particular public works from funding to construction to operations and maintenance. Utilities are similar to independent special assessment districts, such as the Texas road districts, in the autonomy they enjoy. Utilities and independent special assessment districts may be distinguished by their duration, geographical breadth, and functional scope.

As defined here, utilities are given perpetual responsibility to operate and maintain particular public works. They are not created for a limited duration such as the infrastructure construction period. Moreover, a utility is not confined to the neighborhood component of a public works system but includes the whole generating and distribution structure. Finally, a utility does not delegate administrative decisions concerning financing, personnel, etc., to another governmental department; these are handled within the utility, which operates as an independent public corporation.

Characteristically, utilities charge initial hook-up fees for capital expansion plus periodic charges based on actual or presumed use for operations and maintenance. The variables used to calculate each fee depend primarily on the particular public works involved.

There are two advantages in organizing public works as utilities: (1) financial support is user-based and is related to actual use or benefits received, and (2) planning and financial management are not subject to the uncertainties of general revenue budgeting. The disadvantage is public resistance to what they perceive as additional taxes rather than fees in lieu of increased taxes. Also, some observers contend that public works such as water and roads should be funded from general revenues since benefits are related to income level or property value and not the factors upon which utility fees are based--that is, property size, type of dwelling, etc.

PREVIEW OF CASES

Two case studies are included in this section. Cincinnati is of particular interest because it focuses on revitalization of a stormwater system in a central city that is not experiencing rapid growth. Cincinnati's stormwater system had been neglected and needed significant maintenance and repairs; funds were not forthcoming from traditional sources. Fort Collins provides an example of the more traditional utilities in water, sewer, and stormwater plus a less conventional utility for streets and roads. Monthly fees for water and sewer are based on actual or estimated water consumption. Fees for the other two utilities are based on presumed contribution to system burden--stormwater fees are based on land area and use, which presumably determine runoff, and road utility fees are based on front footage and land use, which are assumed to correlate with traffic generation.

In both cases, organization into utilities allows user-based funding of basic public works that is insulated from the uncertainties of the general revenue budget process. Furthermore, financial stability is not dependent upon robust development. Of course, if debt is floated that depends upon an expanded user base for repayment, then financing is subject to the same risks as all development-based funding.

CINCINNATI, OHIO STORMWATER MANAGEMENT UTILITY

SUMMARY

In 1984, the Cincinnati city council established a stormwater utility within the Department of Public Works to administer and manage the city's stormwater system. This action was in response to several problems in the system, most notably the absence of a single city agency responsible for stormwater management, the aging of the infrastructure, and the lack of a sufficient and dependable revenue source specifically tied to the stormwater system. User fees, based on property contribution to runoff, constitute the revenue source of the utility.

Although other jurisdictions have created utilities to manage stormwater and other public works, Cincinnati is especially interesting as a case study because it is a major urban area utility operating independently of its surrounding suburbs and because it is a central city with diminishing population.

BACKGROUND

The City of Cincinnati occupies an area of 78 square miles on the Ohio River. Between 1970 and 1980, population declined nearly 15 percent from 452,524 to 385,457, and the number of occupied housing units declined by approximately 2,000 to 157,677. In this same period, single-person households increased, married-couple family households decreased, and the number of female-headed families increased. Preliminary data for 1985 confirm these trends -- the number of units and their rate of occupancy remained nearly constant while population declined to 368,712, thus evidencing a continued diminution in the number of persons per living unit.

A 1984 report prepared for the city pointed out the aging of the city's general infrastructure: nearly 92 percent of the city was over 50 years old and 31 percent was over 100 years old. With regard to the stormwater system in particular, the report noted that Cincinnati had no effective stormwater management program and that no single city agency was responsible for such management. Problems were manifest in the general deterioration in the stormwater system as shown by the failure to clean the approximately 30,000 inlets on a regular basis, the serious deterioration of many of these inlets, and the more than 10,000 complaints identified on record (no time period was given). In addition, several areas of Cincinnati were still without adequate storm sewers.

The 1984 report identified three main groups of factors contributing to inadequate maintenance and ineffective management of the system:

- **Institutional**: failure to address the issue of stormwater management when the city-operated sewerage and stormwater system was split up and the sewerage component placed under the authority of the Metropolitan Sewer District (MSD).
- **Organizational**: absence of an agency focusing on stormwater system needs.

- **Financial:** lack of an adequate, stable, and publicly acceptable method of funding stormwater programs after the sewer system was moved to the MSD.

The Metropolitan Sewer District was established in 1968 in response to the suburbanization of Hamilton County; its creation facilitated a regionalized approach to sewage collection and treatment. From the inception, stormwater systems were specifically excluded from MSD's realm of responsibility except where sanitary sewer and stormwater systems were combined. Approximately three-fourths of Cincinnati's stormwater runoff is carried in combined stormwater-sewer trunk sewers; thus one fourth of stormwater-carrying capacity plus all collection facilities were left outside the realm of MSD responsibility. Some maintenance of this separate stormwater system was initially provided by the MSD under contract to the city, but budgetary considerations resulted in cancellation of this arrangement and, around 1976, maintenance of these stormwater systems reverted to the Highway Maintenance Division of Public Works.

With the delegation of stormwater maintenance to the Highway Department, the city effectively placed this system in a position subordinate to streets and roadways. Drainage has subtle, pervasive impacts on many municipal operations and systems and many agencies were thus interested in stormwater drainage. None of the concerned agencies, however, were interested in stormwater management as a primary focus and it became an "organizational stepchild." As a result, long-term maintenance, operation, regulation, and replacement needs were not routinely addressed.

Although the stormwater and sanitary sewer systems had been funded by specific revenues when both had been under the city, the stormwater system was left without a specific source of funding when the sewer system was spun off to the MSD. Thus the stormwater system competed with other city programs for general revenues. Because it was a secondary priority in several departments and primary in none, and because cumulative reductions in expenditure are often not felt for several years afterward, funds for the stormwater system were typically among the first cut during budgetary crises. This, plus the general uncertainty associated with annual budgetary allocations, precluded long-term commitments to maintain and upgrade the system.

In response to these organizational and financial needs, and in line with a growing belief in user-funding of services, in 1984 the city council created a Division of Stormwater Management Utility to operate within the Department of Public Works.

PROGRAM CHARACTERISTICS

The stormwater utility created in 1984 was given responsibility to develop and implement stormwater management plans and to manage the full system. To facilitate this, the division was directed to charge a storm drainage fee based on individual property contribution of runoff to the system, benefits enjoyed, and service received. It was suggested that fee collection begin in July 1985.

A number of alternative fee assessment systems were evaluated in the report including several flat-rate structures, variable-rate structures, and combinations of the two. Each alternative rate structure was rated with regard to ten criteria including perceived equity, cost of implementation, revenue capacity, flexibility, and geographic and jurisdictional considerations.

Following the final recommendations of the study, the city council adopted a fee calculation method based on property area and intensity of development. More specifically, monthly stormwater utility fees were defined as a function of three factors:

- **Area Range Number (ARN)**: an indication of lot or parcel size. Lots and parcels are assigned to numbered categories according to square footage. Each category spans a 2,000 square-foot area range; ARN is the number of the category. Thus an ARN of 1 is assigned to all lots with 1 to 2,000 square feet of area, an ARN of 2 to lots in the 2,001-4,000 square foot range, etc.
- **Intensity of Development Factor (IDF)**: an indication of percentage of impervious coverage on a lot or parcel. Eight categories of land use are identified with an associated IDF ranging from 0.05 for park lands to 0.85 for commercial development. The numerical values for each category are based upon engineering standards, review of and application of these standards to local conditions, and analysis of Cincinnati's 1983 photographic land use interpretation study. Multifamily residential properties are given an IDF of 0.60.
- **Monthly Charge per Equivalent Runoff Unit**: the basic monthly charge, set in accordance with the total financial needs of the system and dependent upon the number and type of wastewater system users.

The equivalent runoff unit (ERU) is the denominating unit for calculating fees and estimates the relative volume of runoff expected from each property according to acreage and type of development; a higher ERU indicates higher runoff of stormwater. ERU is generally calculated by multiplying IDF times ARN. There are two exceptions to this calculation. First, undeveloped lands are assigned an IDF of zero regardless of land type. They thus have an ERU value of zero and are not assessed utility fees at the present time. Second, for administrative ease and in the absence of strong reasons to the contrary, one-and two-family residential properties are split into two flat-rate groups depending on whether they have more or less than 10,000 square feet of land. Properties with more than 10,000 square feet of land are assigned flat rate ERUs of 1.4; those with 10,000 or less are assigned ERUs of 1.0.

Given the method for calculating ERUs, it was estimated in 1984 that the Cincinnati utility contains between 319,320 and 390,280 such units. Of these, it is estimated that less than 30 percent are residential units that will pay flat rates. To meet the projected annual revenue requirements of $5.2 million, the necessary charge per ERU was estimated as $1.10-1.34 per month per ERU. The city council established the charge as $1.28 in August, 1984.

The utility fees collected are deposited in a stormwater fund used exclusively for utility division purposes. Delinquent payments are subject to interest charges and constitute a lien upon the real property.

EXPERIENCE

The data base for the stormwater utility is still incomplete. However, the division chose to begin fee collections as planned in July 1985 from a partial base rather than wait until the identifying and calculating of all ERU values. Thus annual income from fees does not reflect the full potential of the system. Approximately $3 million is collected annually from the partial user base.

The Utility Director, Tom Stitt, feels that the program has been well accepted because the effects of improved maintenance and management are already evident. In 1986, the division repaired street inlets and cleaned all of the city's inlets. Heavy rains in September 1986 would normally have resulted in hundreds of complaints of flooding and damage. Instead, because of improved maintenance facilitated by the utility, fewer than 50 complaints were registered. The utility is now turning to long-term capital planning and, specifically, extending the stormwater system to areas of the city now without such drainage facilities.

APPLICABILITY

Other jurisdictions have established utilities in stormwater management as well as for other services. (See, for example, the case study on Fort Collins, Colorado.) Creation of utilities accords well with a growing desire to have beneficiaries pay directly for the service benefits they enjoy and to segregate these revenues to ensure steady and predictable sources of revenues for the maintenance and expansion of related infrastructure.

Fees for stormwater utilities differ from those for the more conventional water and sewer utilities since the latter usually base charges on actual (observed) system use such as water consumed whereas stormwater utilities base fees on presumed use. Because presumed contribution to runoff does not vary from month-to-month with actual weather patterns but is fixed according to land area and use, stormwater fees constitute a steady, predictable revenue stream without the potential for fluctuation inherent in those revenue streams based on month to month demand.

REFERENCES

Thomas A. Stitt
Stormwater Utility Director
Room 445
City Hall
Cincinnati, Ohio 45202
Phone (513) 352-3418

FORT COLLINS, COLORADO PUBLIC WORKS UTILITIES

SUMMARY

Using the principle that costs should be borne by those who benefit from public works, Fort Collins, Colorado has established separate utilities for stormwater, water and sewer, and transportation services. Although other jurisdictions have created utilities for water, sewer, and stormwater activities, Fort Collins is one of the first to administer the street network as a utility.

Each Fort Collins utility charges users for both capital and ongoing costs according to actual use or presumed benefit. The measures used as surrogates to approximate benefit--and hence the fees paid--depend on the individual utility. Under the auspices of the utilities, the city has promoted more cost-effective construction of infrastructure for the future by reimbursing developers for oversizing or building in excess of current needs.

BACKGROUND

The City of Fort Collins is located at the eastern base of the "Front Range" of the Rocky Mountains, 65 miles north of Denver, and serves as a regional trade center for northern Colorado, southern Wyoming, and western Nebraska. Originally an agricultural community, Fort Collins has attracted a growing number of national electronics firms. In 1985, population was slightly over 82,000, up 46 percent from 1975. Of the population over 25 years old, 36 percent had college degrees. Colorado State University is the single largest employer with close to 6,500 employees.

In the financing and support of its public works, the City of Fort Collins adheres to the principle of user funding. Two approaches have been taken, both of which link payments and benefits and insulate public works from the uncertainties of the general budgetary allocation process. First, Fort Collins created individual utilities to manage water, sewer, stormwater, and transportation. Second, in undeveloped areas, Fort Collins created special improvement districts, using special assessments collected from each property owner to fund the infrastructure that will benefit them directly. (A description of special improvement districts is included in the chapter on special districts.) In both instances, therefore, costs are borne by the beneficiaries. In both cases, also, public works finances and planning are independent of fiscal limitations associated with the general revenue budget.

PROGRAM CHARACTERISTICS AND EXPERIENCE

All four Fort Collins utilities are responsible for the operation, management, and maintenance of their respective existing systems. The water, sewer, and stormwater utilities are also responsible for engineering and development of required capital improvements. These utilities were not established simultaneously, nor are the charges assessed on the same basis for each. Nonetheless, the charges for each are related to benefits, using a measure for benefits appropriate to each type of service.

The Stormwater Utility

The framework for the Fort Collins stormwater utility was established with a 1976 ordinance affirming the principles that, first, all real property within a drainage basin benefits from installation of an adequate storm drainage system and that, second, the cost of such installation would therefore be assessed against the real property in the basin. A storm drainage utility board, comprising of seven members appointed by the city council, was created in 1976 representing local engineering, irrigation, and development interests. The board divided the city into ten major drainage basins and developed master plans for each. The ten plans identified over $40 million in capital improvements necessary for effective stormwater management in addition to the substantial annual costs.

In 1980, the city's drainage-related activities were consolidated and, in January 1981, the city began charging property owners a monthly utility fee to fund operations, maintenance, and administration. This fee is paid by all developed property within the city along with other monthly utility charges. The 1981 revenues from these fees totaled $360,000. Fees are based on two factors: total property area and land-use characteristics (commercial, single-family residential, multifamily, etc.). The fee for each property varies according to runoff coefficient for that property and the operation and maintenance costs in the particular drainage basin to which the property belongs. The runoff coefficient is a measure of surface resistance to storm waterflow; the higher the coefficient the greater is the runoff expected (thus the runoff coefficient of parkland is low and that of high density development is high). The 1982 fee for the average single-family residence was $1.14/month.

Capital improvements are also financed on the principle that fees should be proportional to each property's contribution to stormwater runoff. Improvements required to correct existing problems are assumed to be the responsibility of current and future owners. Residents of three of the ten basins began paying capital improvement fees in January 1982; fees for six additional basins became effective a year later. The initial fees for a single-family residence ranged from $0.33 to $0.81 per month. In addition to the monthly fees, one-time capital improvement or basin fees are assessed on new developments, ranging from $1,200 to $2,000 per acre initially; fees will be reviewed and adjusted periodically in line with financial changes.

Water and Sewer Utilities

Similar to the stormwater utility, the water and sewer utilities assess both regular monthly charges that reflect current use and one-time charges related to investment necessitated by new developments. Rates vary with location (inside or outside the city), land use (commercial, one-family, two-family, or multifamily residential), and, for residential property within the city, whether it is metered or not. Metered residences are charged according to the type of residence and amount of water used; for example, a single-family residence is charged $9.76 for the first 2,000 gallons and $0.81 for each 1,000 gallons used monthly.

Sewer fees are a flat rate per unit with rates set according to type of residence: for example, a single-family residence is charged $10.83 per month. Non-metered residences pay a flat rate per unit plus an additional (fixed) fee based on property lot size for water; sewer fees are a flat rate per unit. Metered properties inside the city pay less per gallon for water and per unit for sewer. Commercial properties pay for water consumed. Sewer charges are the greater of two alternatives: a flat rate that varies according to meter size or a unit charge of $1.44 per 1,000 gallons outside the city and $0.96 per 1,000 gallons inside the city (1986 fees).

New developments are assessed one-time sewer plant and water plant investment fees which are paid at the time the building permit is issued. Residential properties were assessed sewer plant investment fees of $1,600 for the first living unit per building and $1,165 per additional unit per structure as of January 1985. Non-residential units fees ranged in 1985 from $1,600 for a three-fourths-inch meter to $53,100 for a 6-inch meter. Water plant investment fees for residential developments ranged from a single-family unit charge of $300 plus $0.22 per square foot of lot area for those without commonly owned areas to a multifamily unit charge of $1,600 plus $400 per living unit for developments with commonly owned areas. Non-residential developments were assessed fees ranging from $2,000 to above $50,000, depending on service size.

Oversizing

Under the auspices of the water and sewer utilities, the Fort Collins government also promotes long-term, cost-effective construction of infrastructure anticipated for the future by reimbursing developers for "oversizing." Each Fort Collins developer is responsible for the water and sewer lines required to adequately service his particular development. Often, however, future developments are expected to feed into the same lines as they are completed. The city estimates water and sewer line capacity required to satisfy this anticipated future demand and requires developers to install lines sufficient in diameter to meet this demand. Thus the developer constructs water/sewer lines larger than those required for his individual project.

The city then reimburses developers for oversizing costs: the increment over the amount just sufficient to service the individual development's needs. The city thus ensures that infrastructure does not need to be rebuilt in the future as new developments are completed. The oversizing costs incurred by the city are included in the plant investment fee charged to all developers on a system-wide basis. In the end, the developer constructing the lines pays for his "fair share" of the infrastructure, that is, the water and sewer lines necessary to service his development and a portion of the oversizing costs via the plant investment fees paid to the city.

Fort Collins has formalized the procedure and payments for oversizing. The developer must obtain bids from three qualified contractors for construction of the water and sewer lines. The city reimburses the developer a fixed percentage of the accepted construction cost, the percentage depending on the degree of oversizing required. For example, if a given development itself would require a 10-inch line but the city determines that future developments justify installation of a 21-inch line, the city reimburses the developer for 65 percent of the line's construction. Oversizing from 18 to 21 inches calls for the city to pay 22 percent of the sewer line cost. The city's portion of total costs for oversized water lines as compared to sewer lines is greater for some sizes, less for others. These proportions are based on ratios of actual construction costs and estimated costs from engineering cost guides.

Transportation Utility

Established in early 1984, transportation is the most recent of the Fort Collins utilities. With 255 miles of streets and with insufficient revenues from motor fuel taxes and other vehicle user fees to maintain local streets and other minor transportation needs, Fort Collins was one of the first cities to adopt a transportation utility fee system. The fees, included in the consolidated monthly bill for all utilities, are based upon the amount of street frontage for each property and a traffic generation factor assigned to each use category.

When the utility was established, a local traffic generation study had not yet been done. Thus, subjective factors are being used until more definitive data can be obtained. The traffic generation factor varies by land use, equaling 1.00 for a single-family residential unit, 0.65 for each unit of a multifamily residential development, and 4.00 for each non-residential unit. The monthly fee is calculated as the base rate times the frontage, multiplied by the traffic generation factor for that type of property. The average homeowner's monthly charge is estimated as $1.00-1.50 with a minimum fee of $0.75. Single-family properties fronting on more than one street pay on only half their frontage and there are refund programs for low-income, elderly, and handicapped occupants. (For another example of fees to finance transportation infrastructure, see the case study of the Upper Merion Township Transportation Development District.) In its brochure introducing the fee, the city points out that the transportation utility fee is not a tax since it is based on (presumed) use of transportation whereas a tax is related to value of property, income, or sales. At its inception, the city expected to receive $400,000-$425,000 annually from the fee.

APPLICABILITY

Fort Collins' extension of utilities to stormwater and streets indicates that this approach is suitable for more than water and sewerage. Use of utilities in these less traditional areas, however, poses a new problem. Whereas water supply and sewerage fees are based on actual use, fees for stormwater and roads are based on presumed benefit calculated on the basis of physical property characteristics. It may be more difficult to gain public acceptance of these fees than those based on actual use. And, in general, any new fees may be perceived as additional taxes rather than the purchase of a product, particularly for the street utility. There may be legal constraints on the kinds of public works that can be organized as utilities in some jurisdictions. Nonetheless creation of utilities to finance public works is probably limited by public opinion more than legal opinion. Critical to acceptance is an appropriate definition of benefits, and a clear relationship between benefits and fees via consumption which can be measured or suitable proxies.

REFERENCES

Rich Shannon
Utilities Director
P.O. Box 580
Fort Collins, Colorado 80522
Phone (303) 221-6701

112

VI. PRIVATE-PUBLIC AND EQUITY ARRANGEMENTS

This section covers eight cases in which private and public interests share ownership or some of the characteristics of ownership. Loosely defined, this section deals with cases of private equity in public works and public equity in private undertakings. Several types of equity arrangements are covered: public equity or equity-like participation in private ventures in return for public services or property; private equity public works with or without active involvement by the private entity.

PREVIEW OF CASES

Public equity or equity-like involvement in private undertakings is a less common approach to generating income for local government responsibilities. Characteristically, a public political unit (municipality or the like) receives income from a private venture based upon the gross or net revenues of the venture. This income repays property purchased by the government or public services rendered. The first case presented in this section describes an arrangement in Oxnard, California, between the local development authority as agent for the city and a private hotel. The city-funded costs of land purchase and improvement are covered by payments to the city of a portion of the hotel's gross receipts. Government thus becomes a de facto partner in the private profit-making project in return for its aid in establishing the project.

Private equity in public works can be separated into two groups: active or passive. **Active private participation** can include direct private investment and administration of a basically public responsibility such as the Babylon solid waste processing plant in which a private firm contributed part of the initial capital and fully administers the leased facility under the city's guidance.

Active private participation can be even more extensive, as in the case of the proposed Front Range Transportation Corridor in which a private group is organizing the initial engineering and financial effort and funding will be from private payments for use of the corridor. There is no formal participation by public officials or governments in this project.

There are several types of **passive private participation** in public works. First, private equity in public works can take the form of private capital contribution in exchange for contractually defined rights to use of the public works being constructed. Three such cases are described here: Escondido, California, sewer and water access rights; Houston, Texas wastewater system access rights; and Upper Merion, Pennsylvania, sewer access rights. The cases vary in the time frame for purchase of access rights, the conditions attached to these rights, and the structure of the system being funded.

The second type of passive private participation in that in which the private "owners" are far removed from direct involvement in the infrastructure being funded and are, in fact, investors with only a financial interest in the project. These investors "own" a limited portion of infrastructure through their purchase of certificates of participation or equipment trust certificates, a financial instrument. The infrastructure itself is held by a trustee as collateral, and the infrastructure user repays the debt through lease payments. However, the debt is also secured by the legal obligation of the leasing jurisdiction to include lease payments in the general budget allocations as a primary responsibility; the physical collateral would therefore only be collected if the local jurisdiction were to declare bankruptcy.

The Southern California Rapid Transit Authority used such equipment trust certificates (ETCs) to purchase new buses; Oxnard, California has used certificates of participation to provide initial funding for the land purchase and preparation for a hotel and sports complex with attendant parking areas.

OXNARD, CALIFORNIA
CERTIFICATES OF PARTICIPATION

SUMMARY

The City of Oxnard used both public and private equity arrangements to support a private development venture. This case study is of particular interest because lease payments to the city are based, in part, on gross revenues of a private, for-profit enterprise.

Oxnard issued certificates of participation to finance land acquisition and infrastructure construction for a sports facility and hotel to serve as the summer training site for the Los Angeles Raiders football team. These were secured by two separate lease payments from the developer: a ground lease and a public improvements lease. Lease payments for the city-funded public improvements were set as a flat annual fee. Ground lease payments were set as the greater of either a flat fee or a composite percentage of the gross revenues of the facility, the latter giving Oxnard in essence an element of equity participation in the project.

BACKGROUND

Oxnard is located approximately 60 miles north of Los Angeles and 35 miles south of Santa Barbara in western Ventura County. Population grew rapidly in the decade 1960-1970, from slightly over 40,000 to over 70,000, and then continued to increase at a declining rate, reaching 121,100 in 1984. When it was founded in 1898, Oxnard was the site of the largest beet sugar refinery in the world. Agriculture is still important to Ventura County's economy; in 1984, agriculture accounted for $580 million in production and employed approximately 8 percent of the area's active wage and salary workers. Retail trade and services each accounted for 19 percent of the county's employment; government and manufacturing employed 20 percent and 14 percent, respectively, of the area's workers. Two of the largest industrial employers in the Oxnard area are food processing companies.

In April 1985, the Oxnard city council approved an agreement with the Los Angeles Raiders to establish a permanent summer training camp in Oxnard. The agreement called for the city to (1) assemble land adjacent to the River Ridge Golf Course for development and construction of a hotel resort facility and other land necessary to meet the Raiders' requirements, (2) select a developer/operator for the resort hotel, and (3) make every attempt to have the construction of at least 70 rooms completed by July 1986, with the complete hotel open by July 1987.

The city already owned 3.13 acres adjacent to the golf course and proposed to purchase an additional 12.3 acres for the resort hotel. Payment to the current owner did not have to be made before March 1987; the original agreement specified that payment could take one or more of several forms: cash, trade of city-owned property, or credit toward development fees. In fact, payment was in cash. The city expanded this project's financing to include funds to expand the city's wastewater treatment plant and equipment yard.

PROGRAM CHARACTERISTICS

In 1985, the existing Oxnard Public Facilities Corporation (PFC) issued two certificates of participation, raising approximately $16 million. Because of constraints on the amount of land that could be included in the certificates, the city funded an additional $450,000 as an "equity" contribution to the project. Together, these sources provided funds for land acquisition and the necessary improvements for the project. Land acquisition costs were approximately $3.75 million.

The PFC contracted with a developer to build the facilities including parking, streets, utilities, and on-site and off-site infrastructure. The PFC then leased all public improvements to the city for an amount equal to the debt service, and the city subleased the improved land to the hotel developer. The certificates are backed by the city's obligation to make lease payments to the PFC. In turn, this lease payment obligation is secured by the city's general revenue stream.

The city's financial lease arrangements with the developer are independent of the certificates of obligation and are not legally earmarked for debt service. The city receives two lease payments from the developer: public improvements lease payments and ground lease payments. The lease payments for the city-funded public improvements are set at $735,000 annually. The ground lease payments are the **greater** of two alternatives: (1) $326,264 per year or (2) a percentage of gross room revenues, food and beverage sales, and all remaining revenue. The specified percentages of gross room revenues and food and beverage sales increase each year and reach their maximum rates in the fifth year (6.25 percent of gross room revenues, 2.5 percent of gross food and beverage sales). In addition, lease payments include 2 percent of telephone charges and 5 percent of gross gift, newsstand, and all remaining revenues.

It was estimated that, by 1988, lease payments based on gross receipts would nearly equal the flat minimum $326,264 and would surpass it in 1989, thus increasing ground lease payments to the city. With lease payments based on sales volumes rather than a flat fee, Oxnard's position is one of a silent partner in which revenue is related to equity share. The city will also reap other fiscal benefits including bed tax revenues and sales tax revenues not specially enacted for this project and thus not pledged to its debt service. By 1990, total hotel and sports facility-related debt service of $1.029 million is anticipated to be more than covered by $0.735 million public improvements lease payments and $0.485 million ground lease payments (city revenue based on a percentage of gross receipts), with an additional $0.587 million in uncommitted revenue gained from bed and sales taxes from the hotel complex.

The certificates of participation also generated funds to acquire land needed to expand the wastewater treatment plant and the equipment yard. The debt servicing for these projects is covered by sewer connection fees and rental rates charged by service operations.

EXPERIENCE

Although the Raiders were not able to occupy the 70 rooms promised by summer 1986, they will move into their quarters in time for the 1987 summer season. The hotel was opened for business in early spring 1987, and by all accounts, the project will fulfill its financial expectations. The private developer has had to rely on short-term financing. He expects, however, that long-term financing for his portion should be forthcoming soon. The problem lay with the fact that the PFC as trustee holds title to the land used for hotel parking. Although the certificates of participation are secured by the full revenue stream of the city, which is pledged to payment of the leases, and the lien would only be called if the city itself went bankrupt and could not meet its lease payments, the existence of any claim on the land made potential lenders uneasy.

APPLICABILITY

The 1986 Tax Reform Act restricts the issue of tax-exempt certificates for projects such as the Oxnard hotel complex in which a private entrepreneur constructs and operates a profit-making venture. Even in 1985, Oxnard was required to issue two separate certificates of participation, one tax-exempt certificate to fund the public facility related portion of the projects (i.e., Raider Park, and the expansion of the wastewater treatment plant and equipment yard) and one handled in the manner of a tax-exempt industrial development bond for the balance of the public parking and hotel facility. If the project were initiated under the Tax Reform Act provisions, the City of Oxnard would most likely issue taxable debt for the parking facility and hotel land portion of the project; tax-exempt debt would still be allowed for the public facility portion of the project. The equity-participation component of the financing would not be affected by the act.

To avoid the risks of underpayment associated with any development project without sacrificing potential gains, Oxnard negotiated a lease with a floor; thus, debt service payments were assured so long as the project functioned. Oxnard hedged -- but did not give up -- its "equity" privileges in a profitable venture.

REFERENCES

Ken Hampian
Assistant to the City Manager
Phone (805) 984-4607

Jim Bemis
Economic Development Officer
Phone (805) 984-4611
City of Oxnard
300 West 3rd Street
Oxnard, California 93030

BABYLON, NEW YORK
PRIVATE EQUITY IN PUBLIC WORKS

SUMMARY

The Town of Babylon, New York, faced the need to implement a long-term plan for disposal of solid waste. The town chose to construct a solid waste recovery plant on town-owned property. The plant was leased to a private operator who added some equity of his own. Construction was funded with proceeds from a tax-exempt bond issue. Revenues pledged to debt servicing are those from the operator's annual operations costs and revenues, including tip fees that are pegged to debt service needs.

BACKGROUND

Babylon, New York, is a town of 54 square miles in the southwest portion of Long Island, east of New York City. It is the fifth most populous town on Long Island, with a 1985 population of 205,593, and has the highest population density in Suffolk County. The town is itself composed of nine communities and three incorporated villages of which West Babylon, Deer Park, and the Village of Lindenhurst are the most populous. The town has strong manufacturing and service sectors that account for over 50 percent of employment.

Solid waste collection services are provided by municipal crews in two villages. Approximately 30 private licensed haulers service the remainder of the town and account for 90 percent of solid waste collection. Maximum fees for the haulers are set by the town board. Disposal is at a landfill owned and operated by the town, with costs covered by tipping fees (presently $24 per ton) and revenues from the town's general fund.

In 1983, New York State passed legislation that precluded landfilling of unprocessed solid waste on Long Island after 1990. Landfill sites off Long Island were considered but rejected as too costly and somewhat uncertain in their long-term availability. In response to stricter controls on solid waste disposal in the area, coupled with fewer landfill sites available, many other Long Island towns began to construct solid waste recovery facilities. However, these will not be available to Babylon and, given past difficulties with regional attempts to solve the problem, Babylon decided to develop its own solid waste recovery system.

PROGRAM CHARACTERISTICS

The Industrial Development Agency of the Town of Babylon issued a tax-exempt revenue bond in 1985 for $88.9 million. The proceeds were used to finance most of the costs to acquire, construct, equip, install, test, and start up a mass-burn solid waste disposal and resource recovery facility capable of burning 750 tons/day of solid waste. A grant of $14 million was provided by the State of New York through its Commissioner of Environmental Quality. The private company chosen to construct and operate the facility provided an additional $17.88 million as its equity participation in the venture.

The solid waste recovery facility is being constructed on a 10-acre site owned by the town, leased to the Industrial Development Agency (IDA), and sub leased until the year 2020 to the private company responsible for construction and operation. Title to the facility itself is technically held by the IDA but, for all practical purposes (including calculation of depreciation for computation of income taxes), the facility operator is the owner. When the bonds are fully repaid, the operator will be able to purchase the facility for a nominal fee and become the owner of record.

The debt service on the bonds is secured by lease payments from the operating company. In turn, the company's revenues are earned from sale of the electricity generated by the mass burn to the Long Island Lighting Company (expected to constitute approximately 40 percent of gross revenues over the first five years), sale of ferrous metals recovered from the waste stream, and service fees collected from the Town of Babylon for waste disposal. A trustee acts as intermediary for payments into and out of the several bond-related funds.

The Town of Babylon is empowered by state law to control and manage all solid waste generated within the town, including the licensing of private haulers, and thus can ensure delivery of the expected tonnage (230,000 tons) to the facility for processing. The Town of Babylon guarantees delivery of at least 225,000 tons of acceptable solid waste annually to the facility, for which it will pay a processing or service fee that is sensitive to debt servicing costs. The monthly service fee, SF, is calculated as:

$$\mathbf{SF = DS + OM + PT - (EC + RMA) + OPB}$$

where:

DS = 1/12th of sinking fund installment payment, principal installment payments, bond interest due;

OM = operating and maintenance expense, initially set at $671,250, with subsequent adjustments based upon the Consumer Price Index;

PT = pass through costs such as taxes and fees imposed by governmental authorities, lease rental costs, landfill disposal fees, and payment of $2.25/ton in lieu of taxes for acceptable waste processed;

EC = energy credit, equal to 90 percent of energy revenues;

RMA = recovered material adjustment (i.e. a portion of certain net profits of the company from the sale of ferrous metals and other process residue); and

OPB = other payments balance, net adjustments owned to the town or the company.

The OM fee is composed of two parts: a base fee of $475,417 and a risk fee of $195,833. The risk fee is an incremental payment to the facility operator in exchange for their assuming the financial risk and responsibility of complying with future regulatory changes affecting plant operations. The service fee and guaranteed tonnage are subject to change if the company can demonstrate that the energy content of the acceptable waste delivered has deviated significantly from the specified range.

It is projected that, in 1989, service fees will account for $8.973 million, of total revenues, electricity sales $5.345 million and net ferrous sales about $800,000. Total facility operating costs are estimated to be $9.680 million, leaving a net revenue of $5.415 million, equal to projected debt service requirements. The service fee is estimated to be slightly below $48/ton in 1989.

EXPERIENCE

The facility is not yet operational, but construction is proceeding on or in advance of schedule. Public acceptance of the project was aided by intensive education of the public highlighting the technical qualifications of the private operator selected and the fact that, after carefully researching the alternative technologies and costs, the most advanced air quality system is being incorporated in the facility.

APPLICABILITY

The 1986 Tax Reform Act has changed some of the conditions applying to public-private cooperation such as the Babylon solid waste processing facility. Although the use of tax-exempt bonds for such arrangements is not precluded under the new law, some of the conditions associated with these issues are more restrictive. First, the maximum amount of private activity bonds (formerly called industrial development bonds) that can be floated by each state has been reduced. Thus, within each state, each private activity project must vie for more limited access to the tax-exempt market. Additionally, there is a 2 percent cap on the amount of funds raised that can be used to pay the costs of the issue itself -- bond counsellors, underwriters, investment bankers, etc. Costs in excess of this limit must now be paid by the municipality from other sources.

Although the Tax Reform Act did set a limit on private equity participation allowed in projects financed through the tax-exempt market, this cap does not apply to solid waste recovery projects (for a project which would be affected by this limit, see the preceding case study on Oxnard, California). However, the private sector's equity contribution to future projects similar to Babylon's will tend to be less since, under the Tax Reform Act, the tax benefits accruing to a private developer/operator will be less due to reduced annual depreciation benefits and the elimination of the investment tax credit.

REFERENCE

Anthony Noto
Town Supervisor
Town of Babylon
200 Sunrise Highway
North Lindenhurst, New York 11757
Phone (516) 957-3072

COLORADO, THE FRONT RANGE TRANSPORTATION CORRIDOR: PRIVATE FUNDING OF INFRASTRUCTURE

SUMMARY

In addition to the E470 Toll Road proposed as the eastern half- beltway around Denver (presented in the chapter on special financing districts), a private toll road has been proposed for the Front Range area east of Denver. A group of Colorado business leaders has proposed building a 210-mile toll road and transportation corridor stretching from Fort Collins to Pueblo, east of the Front Range metro areas. The highway would be a multipurpose transportation corridor to accommodate up to eight lanes of traffic, a high-speed rail line, and space for a water and power utility corridor. The corridor would be financed with bonds retired with toll revenues and utility usage, with revenues from individual lease agreements negotiated with interested corridor users (power, water, gas, fiber optic cable), equity participation by individual contractors working on the corridor's construction, and possibly a public stock offering.

PROGRAM CHARACTERISTICS

The toll road will be designed as a limited access, high-speed route; construction is anticipated to begin in 1988, with the route opening in 1993. Plans call for approximately 20 interchanges, with toll plazas and related customer service facilities. Total cost was originally estimated at $800 million. Subsequent estimates of cost place the total for the rail and highway facility at closer to $1 billion. There have been preliminary discussions about a connector between this tollway and the proposed E-470 beltway.

It is estimated that the proposed toll road would relieve the I-25 corridor of perhaps half of the cars traveling between Denver and Colorado Springs each day. Because the route would bypass the densely populated and congested I-25 corridor, it is felt that there would be substantial advantages for truckers in terms of time and safety, especially those hauling hazardous loads. Given the high-speed design and exemption from state speed limits allowed privately financed facilities, the advantages to commercial and private travel would justify the tolls charged which, in turn, would be used to service the revenue bond debt.

Moreover, it is estimated that railroads using the toll road corridor could realize savings of as much as $80 million annually. The company would charge the railroads a fee to use the track, which would help finance the road. Railroads would save time since there would be no densely populated areas or grade crossings along the route and because the grades and curves would be controlled to allow high-speed travel.

The company is also soliciting participation from communications and utility companies that might want to string pipes, electricity lines, and fiber optic cable along the corridor, thus adding another source of revenue in the form of long-term lease payments. Another 20-25 percent of the estimated construction cost could be financed by the construction companies themselves taking their profit in the form of equity.

EXPERIENCE

This project is still in the planning stages.

APPLICABILITY

Colorado's toll road law, written in 1883, allows private toll road companies and authorizes counties to review and hold hearings on tolls. Individual state laws may preclude construction of similar private toll roads in other areas.

REFERENCES

Ray S. Wells
President, Front Range Toll Road Company
R.S. Wells Corporation
Carrara Place
Suite 150
6200 S. Syracuse Way
Englewood, Colorado 80111
Phone (303) 779-4525

Peter J. Webb
Senior Vice President
William Kostka and Associates
(public relations consultants for the toll road company)
1407 Larimer Square
Denver, Colorado 80202-1797
Phone (303) 623-8421

ESCONDIDO, CALIFORNIA WATER AND SEWER ACCESS RIGHTS

SUMMARY

Escondido, California, was selected as a case study because it was one of the first cities to raise capital funds through the sale of anticipated water and wastewater treatment plant capacity, because it was unique in encouraging purchase of access rights by non-developers, because it guaranteed city repurchase of access rights at specified prices so long as new hook-ups were requested, and because it was so overwhelmingly successful.

In 1982, Escondido's water and wastewater processing facilities were operating at capacity and were unable to fulfill the city's contractual sewer obligation to northern San Diego and its own residents' summer water demands. Forced by state and local voter-imposed constraints to use more innovative financing, the city sold access rights to 50 percent of the planned capacity of the proposed water and wastewater treatment facilities. Funds raised were sufficient to underwrite the full cost of the proposed facilities without additional funding from a public bond issue. Moreover, since the advance sale of access rights to only half the capacity funded construction of the total, revenues from sale of the remaining capacity are an uncommitted reserve which, it is estimated, will be sufficient to fund all future improvements to the water and wastewater systems without recourse to debt or special assessments.

BACKGROUND

Escondido is in San Diego County, 30 miles northeast of San Diego itself. It is considered the hub of the inland North County area and is undergoing significant commercial and industrial expansion particularly in the health service fields, electronics, electrical parts and communication equipment, and biological/medical industries. The largest concentration of non-manufacturing employees is at North County Fair, a regional 1.3-million-square-foot retail mall. In 1986, the population living within the 26-square mile incorporated area of Escondido was 86,861; this represents a 39 percent increase since 1980 and is more than double the 1970 population. Approximately 15,000 people live in the 45 square mile unincorporated portion of the Escondido general planning area.

In 1981-82, the City of Escondido was faced with serious political and financial difficulties. There was disagreement over growth policies; the newly elected mayor resigned after only three months in office, and the city manager and two key department heads also resigned. Proposition 13 and the recession contributed to a city budget in desperate straits; the $15 million general fund was facing a $2.5 million deficit, and the sewer and water fund already had a growing $3 million deficit. With these deficits, the city's bonds were placed into technical default.

Moreover, the city's worn-out, 11 million gallons/day (mgd) sewer plant had a cease and desist order from the state, and the 45 mgd water plant was unable to meet summer demands. In addition, when Escondido was unable to fulfill its contractual obligations to provide sewer services to northern San Diego, a $200 million damage suit was filed against Escondido by the San Diego property interest.

In response, Escondido set up a non-profit corporation to finance the needed water and sewer improvements. The electorate, through a series of referenda, overturned the corporation and essentially precluded the city from using any conventional financing mechanisms.

With options clearly limited, and faced with the need to act, the staff came up with a plan to finance the necessary investments that did not involve fee increases or debt. The system was simple in its conception: sell future capacity in the water and sewer treatment plants and use these proceeds to construct the plants to provide that capacity. Escondido's sewer capacity needs were addressed in early 1982, water capacity a year later.

PROGRAM CHARACTERISTICS

To finance expansion of new treatment facilities, Escondido offered to sell capacity in the proposed water and sewer plants prior to their construction at prices 35 percent below current sewer and water connection fees. Although it was unnecessary in the end, the city had planned to issue bonds to bridge the gap between capital needed for expansion and revenues generated by capacity sales, if approved by the voters in a subsequent referendum.

Capacity or access rights to both facilities were defined in terms of equivalent dwelling units (EDUs), the capacity required to service a conventional single-family residential unit. The right to purchase capacity was not restricted to landowners planning residential or commercial developments. Rather, capacity could be purchased by anyone holding land in the incorporated area of the city or in the general plan area outside city boundaries. However, it was specified that sewer connections could not be guaranteed for purchasers outside the incorporated boundaries as annexation was a condition for access to sewer facilities.

The city considered the sale of connection rights to be similar to the sale of any new product, requiring the proper identification of potential customers and programs to disseminate information to them. A public relations firm was retained to develop promotional materials describing the critical shortage of capacity, encouraging purchase of access rights by landowners and holders of long-term ground leases, and indicating the prices and limitations on purchase. Notices were included in utility bills, commercial advertisements were placed in newspapers and on radio, and notices were mailed to every property owner in the service area as well as every known real estate agent, bank, engineer, architect, and contractor in the area.

To encourage participation in general and that of real estate and development interests in particular, several enticements and guarantees were included in the program:

- A 35 percent discount off current connection fees was granted to program participants purchasing access rights prior to a stated cutoff date;
- Purchasers of access rights were given a "connection right" allowing them to connect to the appropriate utility system at any time in the future (up to the limit of the capacity purchased);
- Participants were guaranteed relief from any future increases in the connection fees;
- Holders of access rights, though not allowed to resell access rights privately, were guaranteed a profit on access rights resold through the city to other landowners;
- Connection rights acquired through the program could be used for any property held by that landowner in the utility service area.

Because the city wanted to protect future options and not preclude development by parties not involved in the access rights sales, only half of the capacity of the proposed treatment plants was offered for sale. Flexibility was also gained through the resale provisions.

For both the sewer and water treatment capacity sales, contracts were specified not as gallons of capacity purchased but, rather, in terms of the number of water and sewer equivalent dwelling units (EDUs) required. Water and sewer EDUs are defined respectively as the average water consumption and average wastewater discharge from a single-family residence. The value in gallons of the water and sewer EDUs purchased under the program are calculated by the city engineer at the time of actual hook-up.

At the time of the capacity sales, a sewer EDU was calculated as 270 gallons of wastewater per day. For the purposes of the program, all multifamily users were assumed to require 0.75 EDUs per unit, and the EDU needs of other users were based on actual flow anticipated by the city engineer.

The city set a target of $12 million to cover the immediate financial needs of the planned 5.5 mgd expansion in plant capacity; it initially agreed to accept applications for capacity at the following specified prices until either the target was met or it issued its final notice of completion for the sewer plant expansion:

Purchases on or before:	Price per EDU
6/30/82	$ 1,500
6/30/83	1,650
6/30/84	1,850
6/30/85	2,250
6/30/86	2,700
6/30/87	3,250

Resales of sewer capacity must be made through the city; the seller is reimbursed according to the above schedule as the capacity rights are allocated to new purchasers. Although the city does not guarantee it will be able to resell access rights, it does guarantee that capacity available for resale will be sold to new buyers before previously uncommitted capacity owned by the city. The most recent (July 1987) price for sewer access rights is $3,600 per EDU. This price is based on the cost of incremental capacity plus the necessary support infrastructure such as oversizing and lift stations.

At the time of the 1983 water capacity sale, the standard water EDU was calculated as 750 gallons per day; multifamily units with maintained yard areas of 400 square feet or less were assumed to require 0.75 EDUs per unit. Single-family dwellings were assumed to require an additional 0.50 EDU per acre for land in excess of one acre.

Water needs for commercial/industrial establishments were calculated on an individual basis except where specified by the city. The accompanying table indicates the basis used to calculate the EDU needs for several types of non-residential purchasers of access rights. Two standards were employed: calculation (1) by type of establishment and capacity and (2) by number of fixtures. Calculation of the water needs of standard commercial establishments such as restaurants, schools, and theatres, for example, used the first standard; calculation of the water needs of other commercial/industrial buildings such as stores, banks, offices, warehouses, and the like were calculated using the second.

Calculation of Industrial/Commercial Needs

By:	**Type of Establishment**	gallons/day
	Restaurants, per seat	35
	Restaurants, 24 hour, per seat	50
	Schools, per student	12
	Theatres, per seat	3
	Laundries, per machine	300
	Motel, per room	100
By:	**Type of fixture**	gallons/day/fixture
	Dental or bar sink, wash basin, drinking fountain	14
	Floor drain, urinal	28
	Commercial sink, service sink	42
	Toilet	56

The city planned to double water treatment capacity and, to finance this expansion, offered to sell rights to future capacity until it received commitments for 29,000 EDUs or until May 20, 1983. Given the timely response a year earlier to the sewer access rights offering, the time frame for water capacity rights was limited from the outset to a three-month period with the price at $900/EDU until the May cutoff, increasing to $1,500/EDU the next day.

As in the sewer capacity rights program, water access rights can be resold only through the city. The sellers will be reimbursed according to the following schedule as long as there are landowners interested in purchasing capacity:

Returns on or before:	Amount remitted per EDU
7/1/84	$1,200
7/1/85	1,380
7/1/86	1,590
7/1/87	1,825
after 7/1/87	about 10 percent more each year

The current (1987) purchase price for water access rights is $2,400/EDU; this is based on the cost of new plant capacity and necessary infrastructure including oversizing.

Under both the sewer and water access rights programs, purchasers could secure their rights with letters of credit, thus allowing them to space their cash flows.

EXPERIENCE

Three months were spent on capacity sales for each project; a total of $26 million was raised for both projects at a total cost (including staff time) of $60,000. This revenue exceeded initial targets by $8 million; both projects were thus fully funded, and the residual is available for other capital projects. Approximately 10-12 percent of the sewer access rights sold were purchased by non-developers. Most of these were residents in septic system areas securing access in anticipation of future annexation. Of the water access rights sold, approximately 20 percent were purchased by non-developers, either by residents on well water anticipating annexation or by investors (holding land in Escondido) attracted by the guaranteed resale prices.

The city estimates that it has gained $1 million in added income through the repurchase and resale of access rights. Approximately 10 percent of sewer and 20 percent of water access rights have been resold through the city. Some of these transfers were due to developers who, upon selling their properties to other developers, chose for financial reasons to transfer the access rights via the city's repurchase/resale plan rather than convey the rights directly to the new owners.

It is estimated that future connection fees, which are not required to pay off debt on the current capacity, will generate another $100 million over the next 20 years. This means that future infrastructure can be financed with cash on hand, thus eliminating the need and cost of public debt.

An additional benefit has been the restoration of public confidence in the city's local government. The program received strong support from both the business and development community and the managed growth interests; program participants and general citizenry have also been supportive. Opposition has come only from those opposed to growth in general since the program has, of course, eliminated barriers to growth.

APPLICABILITY

Other communities have already adopted programs similar to Escondido's sale of access rights; see, for example, case studies on Houston and Upper Merion Township described elsewhere. Use of this fund-raising technique, however, does require fairly strong local demand for new treatment capacity and a general willingness to cope with the problems of growth through development plans rather than sewer moratoriums. Clearly, this type of program is applicable only to infrastructure to which access can be controlled and restricted to those fulfilling certain entry conditions.

During the two sale periods, Escondido reserved the right to rescind the sales and refund the proceeds if response was insufficient to fund most of the planned expansions. Thus, although there were risks from insufficient capacity and the pending lawsuit, programs such as Escondido's can be structured so that there is no financial risk to the community from the allocation of nonexistent future capacity as all commitments can be nullified within a stated time period. Communities not restricted as Escondido was in its ability to float bonds can use a combination of bonding and the sale of access rights to fund capacity expansions.

REFERENCES

Roderick J. Wood
Assistant City Manager of Escondido
100 Valley Boulevard
Escondido, California 92025
Phone (619) 741-4631

HOUSTON, TEXAS
WASTEWATER SYSTEM ACCESS RIGHTS

SUMMARY

In response to a shortfall in wastewater treatment capacity, coupled with insufficient revenues from historical sources of investment funds, the Houston city council created a new source of wastewater investment funds based on capital recovery charges (CRCs). CRCs are one-time fees, similar to impact fees, collected from new users requesting access to the system and from old users requiring increases in capacity. In exchange for payment of the CRC, applicants are guaranteed future access to a contracted amount of system capacity that has been reserved for their use.

BACKGROUND

The Houston sewer system has 372,400 active service connections serving 1.9 million people. There are 49 wastewater treatment plants and 3 sludge treatment facilities processing an average daily flow of approximately 250 million gallons.

The City of Houston's sanitary sewer system was established in 1976 as a self-supporting enterprise fund financed primarily through sewer service charges. At that time, the system initiated a major program of capital improvements and enhancements to treatment plant capacity, wastewater collection lines, lift stations, and sludge disposal facilities to remedy a capacity shortfall. In spite of this, the demands for wastewater treatment capacity associated with the construction boom of the late 1970s and early 1980s outpaced the system's capacity.

Because of this shortfall in capacity, land development was subject to building moratoriums or severe restrictions in large portions of the city. Simultaneously, it was projected that reduced availability of federal funds would severely restrict future expansion. (Between 1976 and 1986, almost half of the $800 million expended on the sewer capital plan came from the U.S. Environmental Protection Agency Construction Grants Program.)

The city council was faced with three alternatives: limiting development, increasing the financial burden on established users of the system, or finding new sources of funds for expansion. While rejecting the choice to restrict development, the council was reluctant to increase the level of revenue bonds issued or to escalate sewer rates for existing customers. The council felt it was more equitable to place the financial burden of new capacity primarily on the new customers creating the need for such expansion. Thus, the city council opted to create a new revenue source for capital funding derived from fees levied against new entrants into the system.

In May 1983, the city council passed the Capital Recovery Charges (CRC) Ordinance mandating the collection of one-time charges for new connections or increased use through existing connections. The council felt that this system would also provide greater security to developers than other financing options by guaranteeing wastewater treatment capacity to builders who paid the CRC fees, thus insuring them against any sewer moratoriums that might be declared.

PROGRAM CHARACTERISTICS

Builders seeking a building permit must first submit to the wasteload control staff of the Department of Public Works an estimate of the daily wastewater discharge to be expected from the new project when completed. The staff first determines if the system has sufficient uncommitted capacity to process the anticipated volume. If sufficient unreserved capacity is available, the staff calculates the CRC for the projected discharge, the applicant pays the CRC, and applies for the building permit. The wastewater system staff then reserves the necessary wastewater treatment capacity for the future use of the individual applicant's project; this capacity is subtracted from the capacity available for future allocation, thus reducing the unclaimed capacity available to later applicants. If sufficient capacity is unavailable, the building permit is denied and the builder must defer his project until new capacity is built or capacity is released by someone with unused access rights.

Payment of the CRC does not in any way guarantee the applicant a building permit; it is only the first of several steps, and the applicant must satisfy all other conditions for building permits as well. Furthermore, payment of the CRC does not exempt the builder from payment of tap or connection fees; connection fees are paid at the time of hookup. (For comparison, see the case study on sewer access rights in Upper Merion Township, Pennsylvania, where the comparable access fee is much higher than Houston's CRC but separate connection fees have been eliminated.)

If the director of the Department of Public Works and Engineering determines that a particular wastewater facility is operating at 85 percent of its legally permitted capacity and that increased allocations of capacity would result in an overloading, then restrictions are imposed upon further utility connections in that area. However, applicants requiring less than 1,575 gallons per day per acre (typical for residential customers) are exempt from these restrictions.

The wastewater treatment capacity reserved when the CRC is paid is specified in an enforceable written contract between the city and the party acquiring the reservation. The capacity thus allocated is transferrable to other parties only within the same service area, after payment of a transfer fee, and only with the express approval of the system's director. The director's approval is contingent upon the availability of sufficient capacity in the system to service the needs of the development slated to receive the transferred wastewater capacity reservation, approval of the technical specifications of the new user, and confirmation that the party giving up capacity will not, in fact, need that capacity.

Because such transfers of access rights are allowed, there is the potential for a "grey market" in wastewater capacity within any one service area since the price of transferred capacity is not controlled, and transfer is not restricted to applicants on a waiting list. (In contrast, see the case study on Upper Merion, Pennsylvania, where no transfers are permitted and excess capacity owned by one user can only be turned back to the wastewater authority.)

The amount of the CRC depends upon the characteristics of the proposed development. If the development is to be served by a completely new connection to the system the CRC is computed as:

$$(A * B) - (C + \$500)$$

where:

A = current dollar per day per gallon charge set by the system as the basis for calculating CRC;

B = average amount of wastewater expressed in gallons per day that is expected to be charged into the system by the proposed development;

C = sum of all capital contributions made by the property owner to the city used to acquire all or a portion of a wastewater facility, including the cash value of in-kind contributions.

If the proposed development is to be served totally or in part through a previously existing connection to the system, the unit charge "A" is assessed only against the increment in gallons per day and the $500 flat-fee is excluded.

All amounts collected as capital recovery charges are maintained as a separate city account and used solely for paying or reimbursing all or a portion of the capital cost of construction of specific facilities designed to increase the capacity of the wastewater system. Such revenues are not available for repairing or replacing existing facilities nor for extending or enlarging sewer mains unless this is ancillary to the operation of new capacity.

In addition to the regular CRC program, the city council also provided for acceleration of capital projects. In areas restricted to single-family residential construction and in which there is a substantial demand for capacity, the wastewater control staff can propose an acceleration in construction of new capacity. The proposed expansion is advertised, and financial commitments or subscriptions are solicited from property owners in the area. These financial subscriptions are essentially CRCs committed earlier than would normally be the case (possibly even prior to specification of an applicant's proposed development). If the subscriptions received are considered sufficient by the director, the relevant facility is moved forward on the capital improvement plant timetable.

EXPERIENCE

At the time the ordinance was passed in 1983, the unit charge "A" used to calculate CRC was set at $1.448; it is currently set at $1.0606 per gallon per day. During the four fiscal years 1983-1986 (FY ending July 1 each year), close to $27 million in CRCs was paid into the CRC fund; an additional $11 million in interest was earned. During the same period, over $41 million was paid into the fund for accelerated projects. These revenues are associated with 47.7 million and 30.5 million gallons per day, respectively, of reserved capacity. Income to both accounts was highest in 1984-5 and dropped substantially in FY 1986.

The Fiscal Administrator of the Houston Public Works Department, John Baldwin, noted that one concomitant of the new program has been a shift away from construction of large-scale new sewage treatment plants to construction of smaller plants located throughout the city that can be expanded in incremental modules as "accelerated projects." Thus there are 50 individual service areas in Houston, each with specified treatment facilities. During the initial years of the CRC method of financing, there appears to have been an easing in sewer restrictions. In October 1984, there were 24 totally restricted service areas; this declined to 15 a year later and to 8 by October 1986. During this same period, partially restricted service areas increased from zero to 17 as restrictions were partially lifted.

Baldwin also noted that there were objections to the CRC program when it was initiated in 1983 and that these objections have not abated but have increased with the recent decline in Houston's economy. Nonetheless, he concluded that CRCs have proved to a viable tool for wastewater capacity financing and, though a review may be called for, neither the mayor nor the city council have revoked their support.

APPLICABILITY

Houston's CRC program for financing expansion in wastewater treatment capacity is similar in many respects to programs relying on impact charges. There is a similar direct relationship between fees paid and benefits received. But, in the case of the CRC program, the benefits are quite specific in quantity and value; the developer is "buying" an explicit treatment capacity. Moreover, the city commits itself to a definite timetable--that is, to having the reserved capacity available when the development project is completed. By relying on this method of financing, the city feels the capital program is subject to fewer delays and uncertainties than if revenue bonds and federal grants were the primary funding sources. And, citing the rationale of all impact-type fees, the city council feels that new users should pay for the impact their entry creates.

The primary disadvantage of a CRC-type program is the same as that of any impact-type fee program, namely, the possible discouragement of new development desired by the jurisdiction. The allocation of the capital burden within the system depends upon how the benefits are perceived to be distributed and whether or not new development will be discouraged by the contemplated fee levels.

A CRC-based program similar to Houston's therefore may be suitable for any area in which impact-type fees are acceptable and in which anticipated new development is expected to overburden the existing wastewater (or water) treatment facilities. Similar programs have already been established in Escondido, California, and Upper Merion Township, Pennsylvania; these systems are also included as case studies in this book.

REFERENCES

John Baldwin, Fiscal Administrator
Department of Public Works
P.O. Box 1562, Room 2417 Annex
Houston, Texas 77251
Phone (713) 247-1418

John Baldwin, "Houston's Capital Recovery Charge System," 1986

UPPER MERION TOWNSHIP, PENNSYLVANIA WASTEWATER ACCESS RIGHTS

SUMMARY

Faced with the need for construction of additional sewage treatment capacity in Upper Merion Township and reluctant to excessively tax present customers, the Municipal Authority and the Township Board of Supervisors created the Upper Merion Municipal Utility Authority Sewer Access Rights Program. Under this program, increased capacity for new customers will be financed in part through a prepurchasing and capacity reservation system in which payment of predetermined fees guarantees access to sewer system services.

BACKGROUND

Upper Merion Township (which includes King of Prussia) is a fast-growing suburb about 15 miles west of Philadelphia. Major roads, including the Pennsylvania Turnpike, Schuylkill Expressway, and Route 202 have made this area a desirable location for residential, industrial, and commercial development. Between 1975 and 1985, the population has grown by 8.47 percent to 28,263.

Given the extensive building activity in the area, it is not surprising that additional sewage treatment capacity is necessary to sustain the continued growth. However, the Utility Authority and the Township Board of Supervisors wanted to minimize cost increases to the present customers, thus precluding capital expansion based on user fees alone. They decided to model the Upper Merion wastewater treatment program after other programs such as the one in Escondido, California, in which new customers pay a form of wastewater impact fees and, by so doing, acquire a right to a given amount of sewer treatment capacity for their developments.

PROGRAM CHARACTERISTICS

Any property owner in Upper Merion wishing to develop or expand existing facilities may apply to the authority for guaranteed sewer access rights for a particular parcel. Payment of the sewer access rights fee is due after the application is approved. Such advance purchase of access does not give the landowner vested rights in obtaining land use approvals; it conveys a right to sewer service upon completion of the development project. The fee paid for sewer access rights is a function of the capacity that is to be set aside and of the costs anticipated for new capacity.

In Upper Merion, additional wastewater treatment capacity is to be constructed in stages; the precise amount to be constructed at each stage will be determined by the amount of capacity requested. Thus, expansion will be in response to quantified demand. Initial estimates indicate a need for an additional 4 million gallons per day of capacity over the coming 5-10 years. Given this estimate, the authority has retained an engineer to design an expansion of one plant that would begin in mid-1987 and be completed by early 1989. In 1985 dollars, the estimated cost of that project is nearly $12 million.

Over the longer term, replacement of an incinerator, anticipated for completion by 1991, is expected to cost $4-5 million; another $23.5 million in 1985 dollars, or $36.5 million in time-of-construction dollars, is expected to be spent on a second treatment capacity expansion slated to be initiated in 1994 and completed in 2003. Adding all these costs in year-of-construction dollars yields a total anticipated capital cost of $54.6 million to provide an additional 4 million gallons per day of capacity. Inflating this by a contingency factor of 1.15 (i.e., increasing the total by 15 percent) yields an expected capital cost of approximately $15.70 per gallon per day of new capacity.

The sewer access fee collected from each applicant is in lieu of a tapping fee and is calculated as

$ Fee = ($3,200) * (number of EDUs)

where EDU or equivalent dwelling unit is the basic unit of consumption, assumed to be 200 gallons per day or the flow equivalent to that of an average single-family residence. The basic charge of $3,200 per EDU was derived as the estimated capital cost of $15.70 multiplied by the EDU flow of 200 gallons per day and rounded up from the computed $3,140. (For comparison, see the case studies on Houston's Capital Recovery Charges Program in which fees charged are $1.606 per gallon per day but other fees are not waived, and Escondido where access rights of 270 gallons per day cost $1,500 in 1982 and other fees were waived.)

The authority has published an explicit list to be used in calculating the number of EDUs associated with each type of development. Calculations are based on space used or expected volume, depending on the type of establishment; the specifications for some uses are detailed in the accompanying table.

If, after connection to the system, the applicant's development uses more gallons per day on the average than were reserved in advance as EDUs, the authority assesses a penalty surcharge on the excess each quarter. In the authority's explanatory brochure and application form, an illustration of surcharge calculation uses $4 per gallon as the penalty assessed each quarter, based on a $16 per gallon per year cost of wastewater treatment.

Once granted, sewer access rights may be transferred only through the authority; no direct sales or transfers are permitted. If property with sewer access rights is sold, however, the rights may be transferred to the new owner subject to approval by the authority.

In the interim before planned expansion is complete, the authority has obtained a limited amount of capacity in a neighboring jurisdiction. Use of this rented capacity, however, requires the payment of charges over and above the sewer rights access fees. These additional costs for interim connections depend on the location of the rented capacity and range from $220 to $400 per EDU.

Calculation of EDUs by property use

EDUs, space calculation basis		
Use	Area or unit	EDUs
Warehouse	10,000 sq.ft.	1.0
Retail store	2,000 sq.ft.	1.0
Commercial and/or office	1,570 sq.ft.	1.0
Motel/hotel	1 room/unit	0.5
Auto service station	1 pumping island	2.5
Hospital	1 room	1.0
EDUs, volume calculation basis		
Use	Unit, assumed gpd	EDUs
Restaurant, regular or fast food	30 gpd/seat	0.15
Hairdressers	57 gpd/chair	0.285
Dentist's office	200 gpd/chair	1.0
Schools (public, private)	30 gpd/person	0.15
Day care schools	22.5 gpd/person	0.113
Self-service laundries	500 gpd/washer	2.5

EXPERIENCE

To date, over 370,000 gallons per day of new capacity have been set aside; of this, 253,000 gallons have been purchased and agreements finalized. Additionally, agreements and financial guarantees for 67,000 gallons of interim capacity are currently being processed. The resulting interim capacity remaining is 50,000 gallons per day.

Bids for the expansion of the Matsunk Water Pollution Control Center were scheduled to be received in August 1987, and the award of a contract expected in September. Once the construction contract is signed, an additional 100,000 gallons of interim capacity will become available.

APPLICABILITY

Programs like this one benefit from the close relationship between those who occasion bottlenecks and those who pay to rectify them. This is true for all the programs in this book based on impact-type assessments; the connection is particularly clear in the sale of water and sewer access rights or processing capacity. Like Houston and Escondido, Upper Merion Township guarantees capacity and therefore the ability to handle new developments as they are finished, yet is not burdening the established population with the costs of growth. And, like the other two cases, reserved capacity and assessments are based on anticipated demand. For a more detailed discussion of the applicability of this mode of financing, see the Houston and Escondido case studies presented above.

REFERENCES

Don Burgess
Project Coordinator

Roman Pronczak
Director of the Wastewater Department
Upper Merion Municipal Utility Authority
175 West Valley Forge Road
King of Prussia, Pennsylvania 19406
Phone (215) 783-7192

LOS ANGELES, CALIFORNIA EQUIPMENT TRUST CERTIFICATES

SUMMARY

The Southern California Rapid Transit District has issued three series of equipment trust certificates to underwrite the costs of a portion of new transit bus purchases. With these certificates, the buses themselves are owned by a trustee on behalf of the certificate purchasers and the bank issuing the supporting letter of credit, and are leased back to the district until the certificates are fully redeemed. The district is responsible for payments to the trustee sufficient to cover all debt interest and principal payments.

BACKGROUND

Los Angeles County encompasses 4,083 square miles and is the most populous county in the nation. The economy is strong and expanding, with a gross county product of over $100 billion a year. It serves as the central trade district for the western United States and is a leader in the communications and manufacturing industries. In 1984, approximately 24 percent of the county's nonagricultural employment was in durable and nondurable goods manufacturing, 23 percent in retail and wholesale trade, 25 percent in services, and 12 percent in government. Despite increasing urbanization, agriculture remains an important sector, generating gross receipts from crops and livestock of approximately $303.2 million (in 1984).

The Southern California Rapid Transit District (SCRTD or the District) is a public corporation providing bus service to a 2,300-square-mile area located primarily within Los Angeles County. The SCRTD operations involve a fleet of 2,770 vehicles handling 1.5 million weekday passenger-boardings over a 5,100 mile system.

Like most public transit systems in United States urban areas, SCRTD farebox revenues are insufficient to cover all of its operating expenses and it relies on federal, state, and local governments for support. In the 1984-1985 fiscal year, intergovernmental sources comprised 68 percent of SCRTD operating revenues. One of SCRTD's principal funding sources is derived from an allocation of sales tax revenues under the Transit Development Act (TDA) of 1971 under which 1/4 of 1 percent of the 6 percent state sales tax is available for public transportation. The SCRTD received TDA funds of over $143 million in the fiscal year that ended June 28, 1986, of which almost $135 million was for operations. A special transactions and use tax of 1/2 cent, proposed by the Los Angeles County Transportation Commission and imposed in mid-1982 after voter approval, has generated over $142 million annually for the SCRTD. An additional $47.5-50.5 million in annual operating subsidies has come from UMTA.

Annual revenues, including various government grants, do not fully cover annual operating expenses even before consideration of depreciation. For example, the shortfalls in fiscal 1984 and 1985 were $0.6 and $1.3 million, respectively. Thus, there are no funds available from surplus or depreciation allocation to cover new capital investments. Such investments must be financed separately through government grants and/or bond issues supported by special allocations and grants.

PROGRAM CHARACTERISTICS

In 1980 and 1984, the SCRTD issued equipment trust certificates to finance the purchase of new transit equipment. As of June 1, 1986, there was approximately $35.5 million outstanding in equipment trust certificates from these issues, which is being repaid with revenues from TDA funds. In 1986, the SCRTD made plans to purchase additional equipment--specifically, 240 transit motorbuses composed of 90 suburban one-door buses and 150 local/suburban two-door buses. UMTA grant funds of $23.28 million were available to cover 80 percent of the total cost of the 150 two-door buses. SCRTD planned to fund the remainder of the proposed acquisition -- 20 percent of the two-door buses plus all 90 one-door buses -- with $3.14 million in available SCRTD funds plus an additional $24.13 million, in tax-exempt equipment trust certificates (ETCs).

However, there was a problem with UMTA's requirement that there be no liens or claims on any buses financed with UMTA funds; that is, issuing ETCs for approximately 20 percent of the value of the 150 two-door buses purchased would require these buses to serve as collateral for the debt and thus would entail a lien on this equipment, in violation of UMTA regulations. This was solved with an accounting agreement that UMTA funds would not be used to finance 80 percent of each of the two-door buses but, rather, would be used to pay the full costs of specific buses representing 80 percent of the costs of the fleet expansion. In other words, 120 buses would be paid for in their entirety by UMTA funds. Thus, buses purchased with UMTA funds would be fully paid for and owned by SCRTD and, therefore, unencumbered. The other 30 two-door buses to be acquired would be financed through equipment trust certificates; they could serve as collateral for those bonds because they would be physically separate from those buses purchased with UMTA funds.

With this administrative solution, tax-exempt equipment trust certificates were issued for $24.13 million on August 1, 1986. The obligations mature over a ten-year period beginning July 1, 1988. The proceeds from this issue, plus the $3.14 million contribution from SCRTD, were allocated to the Purchase Fund for new equipment (approximately $22.39 million), the Collateral Equalization Reserve Fund ($3.44 million), a 5 percent underwriter's discount ($1.21 million), letter of credit ($80,000), and expenses of issuance (somewhat over $160,000). Title to the equipment procured with proceeds from the equipment trust certificates is held in the name of the trustee appointed on behalf of the certificate holders and the bank issuing the letter of credit. The equipment is leased to SCRTD until all principal and interest charges have been paid in full; at that time, SCRTD will acquire title.

The ETCs are general obligations of SCRTD, payable from grants, loans, and revenues of the transportation system **other than** farebox revenues and special benefit assessment revenues. The ETCs are secured in part by the buses purchased with the proceeds of the issue, and in part by cash deposited from the issue itself in the Reserve

Fund, adjusted and maintained over time. There is additional security in a letter of credit expiring when the last ETC is redeemed.

Although revenues from fares are not available to cover debt service on the leased equipment, the revenue from intergovernmental transfers is available as well as investment interest earned and nonfare revenues from advertising and special capital allocations. Repayment of the 1980 and 1984 certificates is from TDA allocations; TDA funds will also be used to repay the 1986 ETCs under a plan approved by the Los Angeles County Transportation Commission. The 1987 fiscal year TDA funds allocation expected by SCRTD specifically for capital needs is $18.5 million; total debt service for all three certificate issues will be approximately $9.1 million, and is thus covered by anticipated TDA revenues.

EXPERIENCE

Repayment of the 1980 and 1984 equipment trust certificates is proceeding without problems and on schedule; no problems are anticipated with the 1986 certificates.

APPLICABILITY

The SCRTD equipment trust certificates are similar to certificates of participation and other debt backed by physical equipment that is leased to the authority issuing the debt. This form of debt differs from general obligation bonds in one very important respect. General obligation bonds are supported by the full taxing power of the issuing jurisdiction, thus obligating the issuer to modify tax rates and policies to repay the debt if other revenue sources are insufficient. Because of this, they require prior voter approval of each issue.

In contrast, certificates pledge revenues based on existing policies and the purchased equipment. They are suitable where the jurisdiction has no taxing authority (e.g., the SCRTD) and/or where voter approval is considered uncertain, administratively cumbersome, or expensive relative to the size of the revenues needed. Certificates can also be preferable to revenue bonds (granted a higher rating and lower interest rate) where revenue streams are erratic (e.g., transit fare revenues), because physical equipment is pledged as collateral in addition to revenues.

Use of such certificates requires that the physical equipment be financed is suitable as collateral and that the issuing jurisdiction is authorized to enter into long-term leases since title to the equipment is held by a trustee until the debt is fully redeemed.

REFERENCE

Michael Butler
Director of Finance
Southern California Rapid Transit District
425 S. Main Street
Los Angeles, California 90013
Phone (213) 972-6581